The Suffragette Bombers

The Suffragette Bombers

Britain's Forgotten Terrorists

Simon Webb

PEN & SWORD
HISTORY

First published in Great Britain in 2014 by
PEN & SWORD HISTORY
An imprint of
Pen & Sword Books Ltd
47 Church Street
Barnsley
South Yorkshire
S70 2AS

ISBN 978-1-78340-064-5

Typeset by Concept, Huddersfield, West Yorkshire, HD4 5JL.
Printed and bound in England by CPI Group (UK) Ltd, Croydon CR0 4YY.

Pen & Sword Books Ltd incorporates the imprints of Pen & Sword Archaeology, Atlas, Aviation, Battleground, Discovery, Family History, History, Maritime, Military, Naval, Politics, Railways, Select, Social History, Transport, True Crime, and Claymore Press, Frontline Books, Leo Cooper, Praetorian Press, Remember When, Seaforth Publishing and Wharncliffe.

For a complete list of Pen & Sword titles please contact
PEN & SWORD BOOKS LIMITED
47 Church Street, Barnsley, South Yorkshire, S70 2AS, England
E-mail: enquiries@pen-and-sword.co.uk
Website: www.pen-and-sword.co.uk

Contents

List of Plates

Acknowledgements

Within the Plate Section images 10 and 11 were sourced from the Library of Congress, while image 17 was originally published in *Punch* magazine.

Introduction

History has been kind to the suffragettes. A century after their activities ended, they are almost universally regarded as having been heroic fighters for a noble and just cause. Hunger strikes, chaining themselves to railings, smashing windows, dying under the hooves of the King's horse at Epsom – these are the images that we associate with the suffragettes. There was another side to their struggle though, and it is one that has been almost wholly forgotten.

In addition to their legitimate political activity and more boisterous protests, they also conducted a widespread and sustained bombing campaign against targets throughout the entire country. These targets included the Bank of England and St Paul's Cathedral in London, theatres in Dublin and the Royal Observatory in Edinburgh, as well as other places as varied and disparate as the Liverpool Cotton Exchange, the Glasgow Botanic Gardens and a barracks in Leeds. The bombings reached a climax in the summer of 1914 with explosions at Westminster Abbey in London, Rosslyn Chapel in Scotland and a cathedral in Ireland.

The combination of high explosive bombs, incendiary devices and letter bombs used by the suffragettes provided the pattern for the IRA campaigns of the 1970s and 1980s. Indeed, the first terrorist bomb to explode in Northern Ireland in the twentieth century, at Lisburn's Christ Church Cathedral, was detonated not by the IRA, but by the suffragettes in August 1914.

Criticising the suffragettes makes many people feel uncomfortable. They were so obviously justified in their anger at being deprived of the vote that it may seem a little small-minded a hundred years later, to be quibbling about the finer details of their methods. After all, the predominant image we have today of the suffragettes is of dedicated women suffering and even being prepared to die for a principle in which they believed, a principle which is today almost universally accepted – that men and women should have equal rights in a democratic society.

At the heart of the popularly accepted narrative about the suffragettes lies two intertwined ideas. The first is that the suffragettes were instrumental in helping British women to gain the vote. The second is that they did so by unconventional, but almost entirely non-violent means. The myth runs that the Pankhursts and their acolyte, Emily Davison, endured hardship and pain themselves in order to draw attention to the injustices of the society in which they lived. They were Victorian women who triumphed in the end by ensuring that it was they, rather than their opponents, who suffered. They sacrificed themselves for the greater good. True, they and some of their more enthusiastic followers might have broken a few windows or trashed pillar boxes, but this was pretty harmless stuff and they wouldn't have dreamed of hurting anybody. When we think of them, it is usually as victims, rather than as aggressors.

Open any book mentioning the suffragettes or visit a museum with a display about them and you are sure to encounter at least two posters created by the suffragette movement which epitomise how we view these women today. The first, entitled 'Torturing Women in Prison', shows a hunger striker being force-fed and the second, a response to the 'Cat and Mouse Act', depicts a lifeless woman in the mouth of a cruel animal. Undoubtedly, these are brilliant pieces of political propaganda; both posters intended to show women as helpless, cruelly mistreated creatures. These are women to whom things are *done*.

The general feeling now is that although these women may have shouted, thrown things, damaged letter boxes and made a nuisance of themselves, they are the ones who suffered and who were the objects of violence and oppression. It was the police who were agressive towards them; the prison authorities who tortured them by force-feeding; the rough crowds of men who taunted and sometimes manhandled them at their public rallies; and the government who played cat and mouse with them.

This archetype of woman as suffering martyr is appealing, in a mawkish and sentimental way, with its selfless heroines who never need to resort to the masculine devices of violence and aggression to get their way. It's a harmless enough fairy tale, as long as we bear in mind that it bears little or no relation to the truth. The reality is very different. Not only were the suffragettes representatives of a profoundly undemocratic and arguably proto-fascist terrorist organisation, it is very likely that their actions delayed, rather than hastened, votes for women.

That the suffragettes were prepared to suffer themselves, and also to inflict suffering upon others, seems a strange idea, running counter to all that we think we know about the campaign for women's votes. So deeply embedded in the national psyche is the notion of suffragettes as tireless campaigners and sometimes selfless martyrs, so powerful is the mythology surrounding them, that one feels instinctively that they could not *really* be described as 'terrorists'. This is certainly the view of almost every modern author who mentions them. Andrew Marr, for instance, writing in *The Making of Modern Britain*, cites one relatively innocuous bomb attack upon an unoccupied house belonging to Lloyd George, and then claims that the suffragettes 'were not terrorists in any serious modern sense'.

It would be interesting to know what people in London's West End would have made of the above assertion if they were among those who happened to be in the vicinity of Trafalgar Square on 5 April 1914. At 10.30pm that evening, a bomb planted by the suffragettes in the Church of St Martin-in-the-Fields exploded, blowing out the windows and showering passers-by with broken glass. The explosion started a fire inside the church and hundreds of people soon flocked to the scene, many voicing their anger at the suffragettes who had carried out this attack.

The best way to consider the true nature of suffragette activity in the years leading up to World War One is to take a few random incidents from that time, transplant them from Edwardian Britain to the present day and then see what we would think of them now.

Imagine for a moment that the leader of a militant group has been jailed. Comrades on the outside decide to mount a protest against the imprisonment by placing two powerful charges of dynamite against the wall of the prison where their leader is being held and then detonating them without warning. The only damage to the prison is the partial demolition of a surrounding wall, but nearby houses have all their windows blown out. Jagged shards of broken glass narrowly miss two young children asleep in their beds. Would this be defined as terrorism?

Or consider this: a bomb is planted in an empty train, which is standing beside a busy railway line. It explodes as another train is passing. The force of the explosion blows apart the carriage in which the bomb had been placed and a beam of wood is hurled into the cab of the other train, nearly killing the driver. Is this terrorism?

A final example should be enough to make the point. Petrol is splashed around the carpets and curtains of a crowded theatre, then set alight. At the same time, several bombs are detonated inside the building. Fortunately, the fires are extinguished before they get too great a hold, disaster is averted, but it is a close thing. Terrorism?

These were not isolated incidents but part of a coordinated campaign of bombings and arson designed to put pressure on the government in Westminster. Such attacks were instigated by the leadership of the Women's Social and Political Union (WSPU), whose members were commonly known as the suffragettes. Paid workers from the organisation were involved in acquiring explosives, transporting them about the country and constructing bombs. It is hard to know what this could possibly be called, other than terrorism.

The definition of terrorism currently used by the British government might help us decide how to describe the activities of the suffragettes. According to this definition, taken from the Terrorism Act 2000, terrorism is:

The use or threat of action designed to influence the government ... to intimidate the public or a section of the public, made for the purpose of advancing a political, religious, racial or ideological cause and involving serious violence against a person, serious damage to property, a threat to a person's life, or a serious risk to the health or safety of the public.

This seems straightforward enough and if you count the planting of bombs in public places, attempts to sabotage the water supply to cities and the destruction by fire and explosives of various churches, railway stations and houses as being serious violence against property undertaken to advance a political course of action, then you will probably accept that some suffragettes were terrorists. When we discover that Emmeline Pankhurst, the leader of the suffragettes, was convicted at the Old Bailey of inciting others to explode a bomb at the house of the Chancellor of the Exchequer, then it is hard to avoid the conclusion that she was in fact the leader of a terrorist group.

The real question to ask is why the first organised terrorist campaign in twentieth century Britain seems to have been airbrushed from history. From attacks on the transport infrastructure and water supply, to the explosion of a bomb at a public hall in Manchester, from letter bombs to politicians and judges to the attempt to flood a valley in the Midlands, this was a ruthless and determined strategy designed to force political change by the constant threat of violence. Books on the suffragettes invariably skim over this aspect of the movement, usually making only brief mention of fires in pillar boxes and the breaking of windows. We read about the slashing of a painting in the National Gallery, but know nothing about the planting there of a bomb; we have all read about Emily Davison falling beneath the King's horse at Epsom, but not everybody knows that she initiated a campaign of arson and had earlier that year set off the first terrorist bomb to be exploded in England in the twentieth century.

This ignorance of the true nature of suffragette activity permeates our society. Danny Boyle, the man who choreographed the historical pageant at the opening of the 2012 Olympic Games in London, said that it was inspired by Emily Davison. It is probably fair to say that few of the 25 million or so people in this country and the hundreds of millions in other parts of the world, who watched this spectacular exhibition realise that Emily Davison was a suicidal terrorist bomber! The result of this ignorance is that we are left with a bowdlerised version of history, with many of the suffragettes' activities hidden from view.

While looking at the violent activities of the suffragette movement, we shall also be exploring the thesis that they did more harm than good to the cause of women gaining the parliamentary vote. They were, after all, only one small group working to that end in Edwardian Britain and the other, larger groups were actually achieving more politically than the suffragettes. While the suffragettes were burning down churches and blowing up trains, other women were negotiating patiently for the extension of the franchise. Their efforts bore fruit, but because they made less of a noise than the militants their role tends to be overlooked today.

Some readers might have been taken aback to see the suffragettes described above as an undemocratic and possibly proto-fascist group. This is because just as many of their actions have now been conveniently forgotten, so too has the essential nature of their organisation and the details of what they were actually fighting for. For instance, the Women's Social and Political Union was certainly not hoping to see the vote given to all women. In their literature, they specifically denied that this was their intention and made it clear that they only wanted female ratepayers, property owners and university graduates to be given the right to vote. They were not fighting so that working-class women should be included in the franchise.

Such views bring into question the extent to which we can accept that the suffragettes were fighting for democracy, at least as we think of it today. After all, what would we think of a modern, British political movement whose stated aim was to restrict voting to men and women who owned their own homes or were well educated? Would we think of this as a group fighting for democracy?

Before looking at the women who carried out the bombings and incendiary attacks during 1913 and 1914, we will need to examine Edwardian society in general, thereby placing the suffragettes in context and seeing what it was that made them so different from all the other groups working at that time to acquire the vote for women. In the course of this investigation, it will be necessary to explode a number of myths. We will begin with two of the most deeply rooted of these wholly mistaken ideas. One of these is that at the beginning of the twentieth century, men in Britain had the vote and women did not; the other, that the suffragettes were fighting so that all women might have the vote.

Chapter One

Suffragettes and Suffragists

❛ *The Women's Social and Political Union are NOT asking for a vote for every Woman ...* ❜

(Outline of the aims included in all WSPU publications)

Chapter One

Suffragettes and Suffragists

One of the commonest and strangest misconceptions about the suffragettes is that they were struggling for the right of all women in the United Kingdom to be able to vote in parliamentary elections. In fact, as they made very clear in the booklets, newspapers and pamphlets they published, most suffragettes wanted the vote to be limited only to middle and upper-class women, those who owned property, paid rates or who had attended university. Gaining the vote for working-class women was never their intention. Some socialists at the time, who were working to gain the vote for every adult in the United Kingdom, regardless of gender or social class, remarked that the suffragette slogan should have been not 'Votes for Women', but rather 'Votes for Ladies'!

In the front of their publications the Women's Social and Political Union, whose militant members were known as suffragettes, printed a brief outline of their aims. This began with the firm declaration that 'The Women's Social and Political Union are NOT asking for a vote for every woman, but simply that sex shall cease to be a disqualification for the franchise'.

This could hardly be plainer. The suffragettes were not interested in extending the franchise to working-class women who did not fulfil the property qualifications necessary at that time to be included on the electoral register, they simply wished for those within their own social class to be allowed the vote. To understand why, we must look at who the suffragettes actually were and how they began. We will also need to examine the difference between suffra*gettes* and suffra*gists*.

During the final 30 years or so of the nineteenth century, there was a good deal of agitation in the United Kingdom for political reform which would enable women to vote in parliamentary elections. Those who worked towards this end were known as 'suffragists', this term being formed from the word 'suffrage', the right to vote in elections. These campaigners achieved considerable success, although progress was being made in small increments, rather than in leaps and bounds.

Some women were not content with what they saw as the slow and halting pace of change resulting from the constitutional efforts of the suffragists. In 1903, the middle-class widow of a radical lawyer founded a new group called the Women's Social and Political Union (WSPU). Emmeline Pankhurst, aged 45 at the time, had already been involved in an organisation called The Women's Franchise League and had fallen out with many of the more moderate suffragists as a consequence of her militant ideas. From the beginning, the motto of her

WSPU was 'Deeds, not Words'. It was also the WSPU that came up with the most famous political slogan of the Edwardian Era: 'Votes for Women'.

Members of the WSPU were far more vociferous in their demands than any suffragists had previously been and they were prepared to engage in direct action, instead of merely working patiently behind the scenes. Their demand was for immediate change, not gradual, haphazard and piecemeal progress. The change they wanted was nothing radical, such as the right of all working-class people to vote. It was simply that women should be able to vote on the same terms as men. Many men and women, those in positions of authority, as well as the general public, regarded the predominantly young, women activists of the WSPU as being wild and irresponsible.

On 10 January 1906, the popular newspaper the *Daily Mail* coined a new word to describe this type of campaigner. They called them 'suffragettes', a diminutive term that was meant to be patronising and even faintly insulting; but the women themselves seized upon it and claimed it for their own. In the years following the end of the First World War, the suffragists were almost forgotten and all those who had fought for the right for women to vote in general elections during the years leading up to the outbreak of war in 1914 became known as suffragettes. For many people today, any woman who campaigned for the right of women to vote in Edwardian Britain must, by definition, have been a suffragette. This is in spite of the fact that the vast and overwhelming majority of women working peacefully for a change in the law were not suffragettes at all, but suffragists, people who restricted themselves to lawful and constitutional methods.

Before we examine further the story of the struggle for female emancipation, let us look at some of the many misunderstandings that have emerged. The following is typical of the narrative that is widely accepted by most people in this country today:

> *At the beginning of the twentieth century men in the United Kingdom had the vote and women did not. The government and parliament were opposed to the idea of women voting and refused to listen to reason. Many brave women were therefore forced to take action to call attention to the injustice of the situation. These people were called suffragettes. Their actions included breaking windows and going on hunger strike. One dedicated woman, Emily Davison, even gave her life for the cause of women's suffrage. Eventually, the movement for change became so*

widespread and powerful that it could no longer be ignored. As a consequence of the suffragettes' actions, together with the work that women did during the war, the vote was granted to women in 1918. We have Emmeline Pankhurst and her suffragettes to thank for this.

The above account is a pretty standard one and may be found not only in schoolbooks but also in many modern reference books. Here is a random example, taken from *The Oxford Dictionary of English*, second edition, revised in 2005:

Suffragette – a woman seeking the right to vote through organised protest. In the UK in the early 20th century the suffragettes initiated a campaign of demonstrations and militant action, under the leadership of the Pankhursts, after the repeated defeat of women's suffrage bills in Parliament. In 1918 they won the vote for women over the age of 30 and 10 years later were given full equality with men in voting rights.

There is no doubt here who is responsible for women gaining the vote in this country – it was all down to the Pankhursts and their supporters, the suffragettes. Perhaps if we work our way methodically through some of the confusion which has grown up around the struggle for women's suffrage in this country, it will help us to understand what motivated them. It might also enable us to find out why they felt compelled, unlike all the other women fighting for the franchise, to resort to terrorism. Indeed, no other women's suffrage movement, either in this country or anywhere else in the world, ever felt the need to plant bombs in theatres or to set fire to people's houses in order to gain their ends. This lack of militant action did not appear to harm the prospects for female enfranchisement in those other countries, some of which gave women the vote much earlier than the United Kingdom. Violent action undertaken for this cause was a purely British phenomenon.

It is sometimes assumed that men in this country had the vote at the beginning of the twentieth century, while women did not. In fact, the situation with regard to voting in this country at the time that the WSPU was founded in 1903 was not at all straightforward. Following the Reform and Redistribution Acts of 1884–1885, the right to vote in parliamentary elections had been granted to some men in the United Kingdom – those who fulfilled certain property and residence qualifications or those who had attended university. What this meant in practice was that when the Pankhursts set up the WSPU over a third of men in England and Wales did not have the right to vote in general elections. In Scotland, the proportion unable to vote in general elections was higher – around 40 per cent. The state of affairs in Ireland was worst of all, with only half of male citizens entitled to vote.

Although women could not vote in general elections, some had been able to vote in local elections since the passing of the 1869 Municipal Franchise Act. The following year, women became eligible to vote for and serve on the new School Boards. From 1875, women could be Poor Law Guardians and when County Councils were established in 1888, women were also able to vote in those elections. In 1892, it was ruled that women could be elected to County Councils, with the word 'man' in the relevant legislation being interpreted to refer also to women.

By the turn of the century in 1900, around 1,500 women held elected office in England and Wales, 1,000 as Poor Law Guardians, 300 as members of school boards and perhaps 200 district councillors.

As can be seen, the position regarding the franchise was far more complicated than is often thought. Some women were able to vote and hold office, while conversely over a third of men were unable to do so. Actually, the voting system contained even more startling anomalies than those which denied over a third of men, as well as all women, the vote in parliamentary elections. While many men had no vote, others had two! Plural votes were not finally abolished in this country until after the Second World War. Take the MPs for the older universities, for instance. Oxford and Cambridge universities each returned two MPs and those who had attended the universities were able to vote there, as well as in the constituency in which they lived. This meant that a man might be able to cast two votes and be represented by no fewer than three MPs. Plural voting of this sort lingered on until 1950.

The electoral system was a mess during the Edwardian period and nobody denied that it needed to be reformed. The debate centred partly around the most just and equitable way to go about doing so and partly upon how the different political parties could gain the greatest advantage from any change in the franchise. There was also the little matter of getting a change in the law through parliament which, before 1911, was not always easy.

Actually, the legislation around voting and elections was so confusing and unclear that it was not even certain until relatively late in the nineteenth century that women *didn't* have the right to vote in parliamentary elections. This led to a series of extraordinary events in the late 1860s. It is customary to claim that women were first permitted to vote in general elections in 1918, after the end of the First World War, but this is not true. As a matter of fact, the first woman to vote in a parliamentary election in this country did so over half a century earlier, in 1867!

In the autumn of 1867, Mrs Lily Maxwell was the proprietor of a kitchenware shop in Manchester. Because she was a ratepayer, an unusual circumstance at that time for a woman, she found herself placed on the electoral register. She duly voted in the by-election held on 26 November 1867. This was before the introduction of the secret ballot, at a time when voters had to declare their vote publicly and there was some uncertainty as to how a woman voter would be received. In the event, Mrs Maxwell's spoken vote for the Liberal candidate was received with cheers and applause from all the men present. Nobody suggested that she should not be voting and every-one at the hustings appeared perfectly content with the situation.

This was very encouraging for those interested in women's suffrage and before the General Election of 1868, a number of female ratepayers had their names placed on the electoral register. Women voted openly during the election, both in Manchester and London, once again with nobody raising any objection. It began to look as though the franchise might have been won for women. However, an official decided to seek a ruling on women voters and on 9 November 1869, the Court of Common Pleas declared the practice illegal. It very nearly came off though, and for a few months it looked as though women had indeed gained the vote.

It is curious to note that there was no large-scale movement in the United Kingdom for male suffrage during the early years of the twentieth century. Most of the men who lacked votes belonged to the working class. They looked to trade unions to represent their interests and were more concerned with such practical matters as working conditions and pay than with being able to vote for this or that MP. In any case, the MP of the constituency in which they lived also repre-sented the interests of those who had no vote.

Many, perhaps most, working-class women had much the same attitude towards suffrage as did the men who lacked the parliamen-tary vote. They were keener to have something done about the length of the working day and safety measures in the factories and mills in which they worked than they were to obtain the franchise. Women's suffrage was an issue of concern mainly to the middle and upper classes. The reason for this was simple. If the law was changed in the way that the WSPU wished it to be and sex was no longer a bar to voting in general elections, then it would make no difference at all to most working-class women. They would still not be able to vote, because they did not fulfil the property and residence qualifications that were needed for them to be on the electoral register. Only the middle- and upper-class women who were agitating for the change in the law would benefit.

It must always be borne in mind that the sort of people who joined the WSPU and became suffragettes, particularly after 1907, tended to be those who hoped to benefit from a simple change in the law, which would give them the same rights as male householders and university graduates. This meant that suffragettes were more likely to come from well-to-do families. For instance, once suffragette militancy was under way, the police complained that they were often outwitted by the suffragette bombers and arsonists because they were using fast cars and high-powered motor bikes. Quite a few of the police reports on bombings and fires mention that motor cars had been heard roaring away from the scene. A hundred years ago, only the very wealthy were likely to have access to a car. Special Branch detectives said that sometimes suffragettes were evading pursuit by switching from one car to another. That teams of bombers could be operating with multiple motor vehicles suggests that money was no object to some of those involved.

There is also the matter of the way in which the WSPU was funded. In 1908, the Labour Party, which was beginning to take off politically, had an annual income of just £9,674. This money was raised from working men and women, who paid small subscriptions. The WSPU, by comparison, had an income in 1909 of £21,213 – over twice as much as the Labour Party. On the whole, this did not come from the shilling payments of those who joined, but was given in the form of large donations by wealthy sponsors. This was an organisation financed by the rich and powerful. A glance at the list of major subscribers to the WSPU is revealing: Lady Wolsely; Viscountess Harberton; Lady Sybil Smith; the Hon. Mrs Hamilton Russell; Muriel, Countess de la Warr; Princess Sophia Dhuleep Singh; the Hon. Mrs Haverfield; Lady Barclay; and Lady Brassey. These were the kind of women who sub-sidised the WSPU and upon whom the very existence of the suffra-gettes depended. A number of these rich women were giving over £1,000 a year, equivalent today to an annual donation of perhaps £80,000.

We have dealt with one widespread misconception – that in Edwardian Britain all men could vote and women could not. Another popular and mistaken idea is that neither the government nor parliament would listen to the perfectly reasonable demands for women to be allowed to vote in general elections and that this obstinacy justified the militant actions of the suffragettes. The argument runs that, having seen the more moderate suffragists exhaust constitutional means, all that remained was direct action. Once again, the facts do not bear out this view. When considering such a proposition, it is important to remember that by the time the twentieth century began, the argument in favour of female suffrage had largely been conceded. A majority of MPs were in favour of women being enfranchised and only the fine details needed to be worked out.

By the 1890s, 340 MPs, a comfortable majority, had pledged their support to enfranchising women. In 1897 the House of Commons passed a women's suffrage motion by a majority of 71 votes. This was not the first time that parliament had indicated its approval of the principle of women's suffrage. Nevertheless, no progress was made in getting any legislation on to the statute book in the next six years. It was this lack of solid results which led Emmeline Pankhurst to found the Women's Social and Political Movement, with the aim of forcing change. Despite the combined efforts of the suffragists and the activities of the WSPU, by the outbreak of war in 1914, women still did not have the right to vote in general elections. Even so, it was fairly plain that women would soon be voting in parliamentary elections; it was only a matter of time.

It must be also borne in mind that women were not in the same state of subjugation in Edwardian Britain as they had been for much of Victoria's reign. There had been dramatic changes in the position of women in this country during the second half of the nineteenth century. For example, a traditional excuse in mid-Victorian Britain for denying women the parliamentary vote was that their brains were in some way inferior to those of men and they would be unable to follow the complex business of politics. Developments in higher education during the latter part of that century militated strongly against such a belief and indeed, in some cases, suggested that the opposite was true and that women could outperform men intellectually. The situation in universities during the final decades of Victoria's reign is interesting in this respect.

London University began accepting women on degree courses in 1878, followed in 1879 by Oxford, with Lady Margaret Hall and Somerville colleges opening in that year. In 1869, a college offering university level tuition for women opened at Hitchin in Hertfordshire. Five years later, it moved to Girton, just outside Cambridge. Students were able then to take Cambridge University examinations. In 1887, a student at Girton College called Aganata Ramsey scored so highly in the Cambridge classical tripos that she was awarded a first class degree. It just so happened that no male student at Cambridge that year managed to get better than a second. This triumph was widely reported and was even the subject of a cartoon in *Punch*.

Nor was Aganata Ramsey the only female student at Cambridge to excel to this extent. In 1890 Phillipa Fawcett, a student at Newnham College whose mother Millicent was to become one of the most prominent suffragists, came top in the mathematical tripos at Cambridge, beating all the men. With women shining at the highest academic levels in this way, it was no longer possible to pretend that the female brain was somehow intellectually inferior and unsuited either to academic study or politics.

As the new century began, even the most die-hard and reactionary politicians probably realised that the world was changing and that the time was approaching when it would no longer be possible to exclude women from the parliamentary franchise. The best that such people could hope for was to fight a rearguard action, delaying women's suffrage and ensuring that when it did appear, it was on the most advantageous grounds for whichever political party they supported.

By the end of Edward VII's reign, women had not only shown that they could compete on equal terms at universities, they were also beginning to make their mark in traditionally male-dominated careers. In 1911 there were, for example, 477 women doctors, with some women also qualifying as dentists, surgeons and architects. In 1913, the first female magistrate was appointed in London. All this, as well as the right of women to vote in local elections and sit as county councillors, had been achieved by the quiet and patient work of dedicated women. They had never found it necessary to smash windows, burn postboxes or throw themselves under racehorses to bring about these advances in the status of women.

As the twentieth century began, there was every hope that the advances made by women in the later years of Victoria's reign would continue and that enfranchisement would be the next development. Anybody looking at what was happening in the rest of the world could see in any case that the time was drawing near when women would enjoy equal democratic rights. It was not necessary even to go beyond the British Isles to identify this trend. The oldest continuously operating parliament in the world – that of the Isle of Man, a self-governing British dependency in the Irish Sea – had already introduced votes for women in 1881. America had been even quicker off the mark; the state of Wyoming enfranchised women in 1869 and by 1896, Idaho, Utah and Colorado had followed suit. New Zealand had allowed women, including Maoris, to vote from 1893 onwards, soon followed by Australia. In Europe, Finland granted the vote to women in 1906 and Norway did the same the following year.

The world was changing and when the incoming Liberal Prime Minister, Henry Campbell-Bannerman, agreed to meet a delegation of women in 1906, soon after coming to office, he told them, 'You have made before the country a conclusive and irresistible case'. Here was the prime minister of a new government who was fully in favour of female enfranchisement. Despite all this, there was still no sign of British women being able to vote in parliamentary elections in the immediate future.

There are several reasons why successive British governments from 1905 to 1914 did not legislate in favour of female suffrage but, whatever the suffragettes claimed, this had little to do with inflexible and sexist intransigence on the part of either prime ministers or the legislature. It is true that Asquith, who was prime minister from 1908 to 1916, was less than enthusiastic about the idea of women voting, but his motives for not promoting the extension of the franchise in this direction were more pragmatic, and to some extent personal, than they were ideological.

To see what was actually going on, and where the suffragettes fit into the picture with their cans of petrol and sticks of dynamite, it will be necessary to examine Edwardian Britain in some detail. The picture that emerges is a surprising one and in many ways counter-intuitive. We often tend to imagine Edwardian Britain as a time of peace and prosperity, the high point of the British Empire. Nothing could be further from the truth and the state of the nation at that time largely explains the lack of progress towards the emancipation of women. For the five years or so that immediately preceded the First World War, the suffragettes themselves shared a great deal of the responsibility for preventing the enfranchisement of women. Had it not been for their activities, it is quite possible that women would have gained the vote before, rather than after the First World War.

Before we look at the state of the nation more widely, it will be helpful to consider briefly the strong element of self-interest with which the major political parties viewed female enfranchisement. The WSPU, which Emmeline Pankhurst started, was fighting for what they called, 'equal suffrage', that is to say, suffrage on the same terms as that granted to men. As we have seen, this would mean that the only women who would be given the vote would be those who passed the property qualification test. Many Liberals and socialists did not care at all for this notion, that only well-off women with property and land should be given the vote. The suffragettes were not calling for all men and women to be given the vote and seemed content for the working classes to continue being disenfranchised.

The other option would be 'universal suffrage'. This would mean giving *everybody*, men and women alike, the vote, regardless of their class or social standing. The consequence of this would be that all working men and women would be able to vote. The WSPU were explicitly opposed to this idea and it led in due course to their falling out with members of the Independent Labour Party, who were enthusiastic proponents of universal suffrage. Full democracy of this sort was never the policy of the Pankhursts and the WSPU.

Introducing 'equal suffrage', for which the suffragettes were fighting, would have benefited the Conservative Party from an electoral perspective, since most of the new voters would be middle- and upper-class. 'Universal suffrage', on the other hand, would probably increase the number of Liberal and Labour voters. The precise proportions by which the various parties might benefit from an extension of the franchise was therefore of crucial importance.

The majority of MPs may well have been in favour of votes for women, but that did not mean that they were about to commit political suicide by creating a huge new tranche of voters likely to vote against them at the next election. We shall look more closely at this question in a later chapter.

As well as the anxiety over who would be supported by the new voters, there were other reasons for the lack of enthusiasm for pushing such electoral changes through parliament, chiefly that from 1905 until the outbreak of war in 1914, Liberal administrations, first under

Campbell-Bannerman and then Asquith, were just too busy with more serious problems to spend time tinkering with the franchise.

The Edwardian era, the years between the end of the century and the outbreak of war in 1914, was a period of turmoil and upheaval, with problems that dwarf anything faced by this country today. It is time to look at a few of the difficulties with which the governments of the day were grappling and this might then give us some understanding as to why altering the electoral system was not considered a major priority.

Chapter Two

The Edwardian World

*❛ **The Great Unrest** ❜*

(Popular term used to refer to the
period of disturbance in 1911)

The suffragettes were a product of Edwardian Britain. This period began with the death of Queen Victoria in 1901 and ended with the death of her son, Edward VII, ten years later; although the term 'Edwardian' is often extended to include the years up to the outbreak of war in 1914. It is the wider definition that will be used here. For many of us today, this age has become a byword for stability and order, the golden heyday of imperial power brought to an abrupt end by the First World War.

In fact, this view is misleading. It was, in fact, a time of chaos and violent change, when the governments of the day faced problems that eclipse anything we see in modern Britain. These included the greatest constitutional crisis for centuries, some of the worst rioting and disorder ever seen on the British mainland, the threat of revolution and the very real possibility of the United Kingdom being engulfed by civil war. Add to this an arms race and severe unemployment, and you begin to see why reformation of the franchise to include women was not top of the agenda for the Liberal administrations which held power at that time.

It is impossible to understand the suffragettes and see where they fitted in during the early part of the twentieth century without knowing what Britain was really like at that time. Unfortunately, the mental image that we have of that era has been so shaped and modified by its representation in popular culture, that this is no easy task. Novels, films and television all too often conspire to present us with a strange and rosy picture, not only of the suffragettes, but also the world in which they operated.

A typical example of the way that Edwardian Britain is treated in films, with powerful and enduring images that seep imperceptibly into our subconscious, is that childhood classic, *Mary Poppins*. This well-known family film sums up both the traditional view of the suffragettes and also of the wider world of Edwardian Britain. Anyone familiar with the film will recall the prosperous and stable world in which it is set. The working-class people in it seem happy enough with their lot; just witness the humorous antics of Bert the chimney sweep and the domestic staff of the Banks household. It is set in London in 1910, but this is not a capital city in the grip of a constitutional crisis which threatens the established order and even calls into question the continued existence of the monarchy.

In the real world of 1910, the country was thought by some to be on the brink of a revolution. In the real world, 12 months after the events shown in *Mary Poppins*, over 12,000 troops were rushed to London and quartered in Hyde Park to protect the capital from unrest by mutinous workers, and men like Bert the chimney sweep were shot down in the streets of British cities by the army.

Mary Poppins also of course features a suffragette, who has her own song, 'Sister Suffragette'. We understand that it is all a bit of a lark, this middle-class wife and mother involving herself in such a business. One really could not imagine Glynis Johns, as Mrs Banks, setting off a bomb or burning down the local church.

Mary Poppins is not alone in the slanted version of history from which we subliminally acquire our image of Edwardian Britain and suffragettes. Think for a moment about television programmes like *Upstairs, Downstairs* or *Downton Abbey*. There is no mention there of warships sailing up the Mersey to suppress a workers' revolt, or anti-Jewish pograms in Wales being dealt with by bayonet charges. We are given to understand that suffragettes were flighty and naively enthusiastic women who might perhaps unfurl a banner or break a window, but nothing worse than that.

It is attitudes such as these that compel writers today, even in the face of all the evidence, to claim that the suffragettes were not 'really' terrorists. They *couldn't* have been – just think of Lady Sybil in *Downton Abbey*, Elizabeth in *Upstairs, Downstairs* or Mrs Banks in *Mary Poppins*. The idea simply conflicts too radically with what people already believe they know about the suffragettes.

An example of this inability to associate the suffragettes with the concept of terrorism was given in the introduction where we encountered Andrew Marr's assertion that the suffragettes 'were not terrorists in any serious modern sense'. This statement appears on the very same page as the description of the partial destruction of the Chancellor of the Exchequer's house by a bomb blast. It would be interesting to know what writers like this would have to say if agents of Al Qaeda blew up the house of a member of the cabinet today. Would they really claim that the bombers 'were not terrorists in any serious modern sense'?

When the Liberal leader Henry Campbell-Bannerman was invited by the King to form a government at the end of 1905, there was considerable optimism among suffragists. Following the landslide victory of the Liberals in the election held the following year, this optimism seemed justifiable. After ten years of inaction by a Conservative government on the question of the franchise, the wind was set fair for change. The only difficulty was that the Liberals themselves had a raft of measures that they hoped to push through, some of them very controversial. Extension of the franchise was not high on this list, Campbell-Bannerman and his cabinet feeling that Old Age Pensions, National Insurance and the first steps towards a welfare state were far more important to those who had voted them in. They were probably right.

As a matter of fact, Campbell-Bannerman himself was in favour of women's suffrage, but that did not mean that he was about to espouse the cause politically. Some of the more impatient suffragists, including those women in the WSPU who would, within a short while, become known as suffragettes, seemed to have a somewhat naïve view of the way that government works in this country. They felt that all the prime minister had to do was announce that something was to be done and it was as good as accomplished. The reality was that Henry Campbell-Bannerman did not have much chance of getting a measure of this sort on to the statute book, even had he been willing to make the attempt.

British prime ministers must, if they are to be effective leaders, win over their cabinets to whatever line they wish to take. Campbell-Bannerman's cabinet was hopelessly divided on the matter of women's suffrage and he did not feel inclined to embark on a fruitless confrontation with the 'antis' in his cabinet. There were more pressing concerns. Even if he and the cabinet were united and able to push such a change through the Commons, it would be almost impossible to persuade the Lords to swallow it. Before the passing of the 1911 Parliament Act, it was impossible to pass any legislation to which the Lords would not consent. The Liberals had seen this with great clarity during the last Liberal government before Campbell-Bannerman's, that of Lord Rosebery in 1894 and 1895. For the whole of Lord Rosebery's premiership, the House of Lords blocked all his domestic legislation, thereby paralysing the government.

In 1908, Campbell-Bannerman was replaced as premier by Herbert Asquith who, unlike Campbell-Bannerman, was staunchly opposed to giving women the parliamentary vote. This excited great animosity towards Asquith and his administration on the part of the WSPU, but made no practical difference to the actual situation. It remained the case that, until 1911, it was quite impossible for any British prime minister to pass a law or establish a budget without the active co-operation of the House of Lords. Had Asquith and his entire cabinet been fanatical and devoted supporters of the women's suffrage movement, they still would not have been able to pass a law giving women the parliamentary vote.

Such subtleties were ignored by the suffragettes and their leaders. For them, the case could hardly be clearer. Those in government who did not agree with their aims or failed to do their utmost to advance the programme of the Women's Social and Political Union were to be treated as enemies. This produced the bizarre state of affairs whereby a dedicated supporter of women's suffrage like David Lloyd George came to be seen by the suffragettes as their *bête noire*. This was perfectly logical if you adopted the world view of women like Christabel Pankhurst. As early as 1903, she wrote, 'There is nothing to choose between an enemy and a friend who does nothing'.

We must now look in some detail at the problems facing British governments in the early part of the twentieth century. This is necessary for two reasons. First, to show how precarious the state of the nation was at that time and why dealing with a series of increasingly dangerous crises was of far greater importance for the country as a whole than worrying about the extension of the franchise. Secondly, we need to appreciate how violence was being used politically, in order to understand why, as soon as the suffragettes turned to terrorism, it became absolutely impossible for the authorities to negotiate further with them or to be seen to be making the least concession to their demands. Various factions within the United Kingdom were trying to sway the government by threatening the use of force and it was vital that such behaviour was shown to achieve nothing and to wring no concessions from the government. Then, as now, surrendering to the demands of terrorists was to set a course for disaster.

In the years leading up to 1914 there was a fear that both revolution and civil war in the British Isles might be just around the corner. It was partly to head off the possibility of widespread civil unrest that the Liberal governments of 1906 and 1910 undertook programmes to tackle poverty and improve the lot of working people. How severe was the threat? During the riots which swept England in 2011, the idea was mooted that the army might need to be called in to control the streets. This was widely regarded as the nuclear option, almost a sign that Armageddon was upon us. It is interesting to note that a century earlier, rioting in England was so ferocious that the government authorised the use not only of troops and armoured cars to contain the disorder, but even brought warships into action to combat the rioting and looting.

In 1911, a year when suffragette militancy was increasing and manifested by window-smashing and hunger strikes, a series of events took place which became known as the Great Unrest, due to the number of strikes, disturbances and riots. Prices and rents were going up, but in real terms wages fell between 1910 and 1912. Many working people were furious about the conspicuous consumption of the wealthy and the ostentation of their wealth – the yachts and extravagant dinner parties, the luxurious motor cars and race horses. The mood among many workers was one of surly discontent and resentment.

The crisis came in August 1911, when hundreds of thousands of men and women were on strike. These were people who worked in vital industries, such as the railways and docks. It was proving impossible to import goods; the ships lay idly at anchor because the dockers would not unload them and the railways were at a standstill in many places. Crowds of strikers gathered in cities and towns, disregarding police orders to move on. The government's solution was the use of troops to support the police.

Throughout July and early August, the number of strikes increased across the whole country. Almost a million workers came out on strike during 1911. Transport workers, seamen, factory hands, railway men – all were striking at different times. The city of Liverpool was one focal point for the unrest. In August, a national strike of seamen began. Other workers in Liverpool came out in sympathy and vast numbers converged on the city centre for a public meeting. A total of 250,000 men and women in the city were now on strike and when an 80,000-strong crowd began marching towards the centre of Liverpool, it looked to the authorities like an attempt to take over the city. Already, the strike committee was virtually running parts of Liverpool, deciding what goods could be moved and which vehicles were allowed on the streets. The strike committee was practically a parallel government, something along the lines of the soviets which emerged during the Russian Revolution. A magistrate read the Riot Act to the crowd, and following that the police, backed by a contingent of cavalry, tried to clear the streets.

There had been no real riot before the police and army attempted to disperse the crowds, but by the time 186 strikers had been hospitalised with various injuries and a hundred or so arrested, the mood had become exceedingly ugly. Windows were smashed, fires were started and makeshift barricades were erected across streets. Armoured cars and troops with fixed bayonets patrolled the streets. It was all a far cry from the world of *Mary Poppins*. Still, the crowds of strikers refused to return to their homes. Incredibly, the government response was to order two warships to sail up the Mersey and train their guns on the city. Armed sailors were landed to secure the docks. Within a few days, there were no fewer than 3,500 soldiers in Liverpool, both infantry and cavalry. The stage was set for the worst confrontation of all.

Just as in the aftermath of the 2011 riots, it was decided that sharp sentences would deter anybody in the future who might be minded to take to the streets and create trouble. Almost all those arrested in Liverpool during the first wave of rioting were convicted of public order offences and sentenced to prison terms. The vans leaving the courts and taking the convicted men to Walton Prison had been assigned an escort of 30 hussars, mounted troops who rode alongside the prison vans to discourage any escapes or attempts to free the men. Angry crowds blocked the way of the vans and bottles and stones began to be thrown at the soldiers. Some of the more daring protesters grabbed at the reins of the cavalry. An officer gave the order to open fire and five men fell to the ground wounded. Two of them, Michael Prendegast and John Sutcliffe, died almost at once, Sutcliffe having been shot in the head twice.

The deaths of the two young men in Liverpool, both of whom were in their twenties, seemed to bring the city to its senses. The government capitulated to the demands of the strikers and the men returned to work. There was a sound tactical reason for the government of Herbert Asquith to capitulate in this way. The fact that the railways had ground to a halt in many places meant, in effect, that it was impossible to move troops from one district to another. There was little chance of bringing reinforcements to where they were most needed. Churchill summed the case up with his usual pithiness, by stating bluntly, 'They have beaten us!'

The disturbances in Liverpool were not the worst that summer. In the Welsh town of Llanelli, troops also opened fire on strikers and in the resulting chaos, six people died. In Tredegar, in South Wales, the first anti-Jewish pogrom in Britain since the Middle Ages took place. Elements of the Somerset Light Infantry and the Worcester Regiment restored order by using bayonet charges through the streets. Cavalry were also used.

While the disorders in the provinces continued, the capital became an armed camp, with troops pouring into London from the main army bases. Hyde Park and other central London parks were given over to the military, and during that summer over 12,000 soldiers were quartered in London. This was a show of force, designed to remind people that the government was backed, ultimately, by the power of guns and bayonets. Soldiers guarded railway stations and patrolled the lines.

It is perhaps hardly surprising that during this particular summer – when the government was struggling desperately to control the streets and prevent what some politicians feared was the precursor to a general workers' uprising – discussing the finer details of the franchise was not at the forefront of the minds of the Prime Minister or Home Secretary.

There is no doubt at that Herbert Asquith, the Prime Minister from 1908 onwards, was personally opposed to granting women the vote, but in fairness to him, it must be observed that he had much on his plate during those years of suffragette militancy. We have looked at some of the problems – industrial action and rioting – which appeared at the time very much like an incipient workers' revolution. It is now time to ask ourselves whether Asquith could actually have given women the vote before 1914, even had he wished to do so.

The Liberal governments from 1905 to 1914 found it very hard to push through some of their legislation, even on subjects they felt very strongly about. This was not fully appreciated at the time and has been all but forgotten today. At the election held in early 1906, the Liberals defeated the Conservatives, gaining 400 seats, compared to the 157 which the Conservatives held. It was a stunning landslide victory and if ever a government in twentieth-century Britain could be said to enjoy a strong mandate, that government was Henry Campbell-Bannerman's administration. The House of Lords, though, was still overwhelmingly dominated by unelected Conservative peers and they were determined to sabotage any Liberal government's reforms of which they disapproved. This obstructionism began with the blocking of the 1906 Education Bill and continued until crisis point was reached in 1909, with the rejection of Lloyd George's 'People's Budget'.

The House of Lords had at this time complete power to meddle in, by either amending or rejecting, any of the legislation coming from the lower chamber. In 1893, for example, the Lords had rejected an Irish Home Rule Bill and there had been nothing at all that the government of the day could do about it. The House of Lords saw it as their duty to oppose any radical changes. When Chancellor of the Exchequer Lloyd George tried to introduce new taxes to pay for Old Age Pensions and other benefits for the poor, the House of Lords refused to pass the budget.

Given the reactionary and intransigent nature of the Upper House in the early part of the twentieth century, we have to ask how they would have reacted to a bill which promised to widen the franchise in this country and give the vote to working-class people or women. The answer is, of course, that they would probably have rejected such a proposal outright. This situation, with a House of Commons unable to rule effectively, led to the greatest constitutional crisis of the twentieth century, which resulted in two general elections in one year; plans to abolish the House of Lords; and even a threat to the institution of the monarchy itself.

It is beyond the scope of the present book to explore this episode in depth and it is probably sufficient to remind readers that between their coming to power in 1905 and the passing of the Parliament Act in 1911, it would very likely have been impossible for the Liberal government to legislate in favour of female suffrage, even had they wished to do so. From 1911 onwards, when they might have been able to extend the franchise, the government's hands were full with other and more desperately urgent matters. Not only that, the actions of the suffragettes themselves ensured that the government could not make any concessions without appearing foolish and weak.

The crisis of 1911, involving widespread strikes and fierce rioting, the likes of which had not been seen in England for a century or more, was bad, but it was not the worst threat facing the government. No sooner had the 'Great Unrest' quietened down a little, than Asquith found the nation quite literally on the verge of civil war.

The civil disorder and industrial unrest had been serious, but an even greater menace to the stability of the United Kingdom was looming. This centred around the demands made in Ireland for Home Rule, and a government of their own in Dublin. The 'Irish Question' had been a thorn in the side of successive British governments for many years. The Liberal government led by Herbert Asquith decided to resolve the matter by granting self-government to this predominantly Catholic island, which had for years been an integral part of the United

Kingdom. This did not please the Protestants in Ulster, who threatened to fight such a move with armed force. Thousands of rifles were
smuggled to Ireland and senior army officers openly sympathised
with the Protestants. The Irish Nationalists were also running guns
into the country and preparing to face their opponents in open
warfare.

In 1913 and 1914, at the height of the suffragette campaign, the
government was therefore faced with the very real prospect of civil
war in Ireland, combined with mutiny in the army and an uncertainty
that officers would obey orders from London. There could hardly have
been a more serious crisis than the threat of civil war and the frag-
mentation of the United Kingdom, and so it is not surprising that
Asquith and his cabinet focused the whole of their attention on this in
1913 and early 1914, rather than tackling the less urgent question of
how and when to extend the franchise.

As if these domestic difficulties were not enough, there was also the
fact that from 1905 onwards, Britain had been engaged in an arms race
with Germany. This entailed both nations frantically rushing to build
bigger and better battleships known as Dreadnoughts, a contest associated with the rise of Germany as an industrial and colonial power and
the consequent menace, as it was then perceived, to Britain's strategic
interests. In 1902 Lord Selborne, First Lord of the Admiralty, said, 'If
the German Fleet becomes superior to ours, the German Army can
conquer this country'. This mistrust of, and rivalry with, Germany
grew steadily during the Edwardian Era, culminating in the war
between Britain and Germany which began in 1914.

Fear of Germany and, in particular, an invasion of Britain by
Germany was a popular theme in books and newspapers in the early
part of the century. Erskine Childers' *The Riddle of the Sands* in 1903 and
William Le Queux's *The Invasion of 1910* both dealt with invasions of
this country by Germany. During the Agadir crisis of 1911 war with
Germany very nearly became a reality, with the British Atlantic Fleet
being ordered to the English Channel in a sabre-rattling exercise.

We have looked at some of the major problems facing the British
government in the years of suffragette militancy, which ran roughly
from 1905 to 1914. There were many other difficulties at that time, all
of which occupied the minds of the prime minister and his cabinet far
more than the finer points of equal or universal suffrage. Something
further to consider is that the problems facing the administrations of
those years often involved the threat of force by factions who wished

to get their own way. No government can afford at such times to be seen as weak and vulnerable to pressure. As soon as the suffragettes began to use violence in pursuance of their cause, they doomed that cause irrevocably. Surrendering to the menace of bombs and arson would, to give one example, have encouraged the paramilitary forces mustering in Ireland to challenge even more vigorously the government in London. Making the government appear weak and apt to surrender to the threat of violence, would have given an unfortunate message to others hoping to force the hand of Asquith's administration.

The portrait of the Edwardian Age, which has been outlined above, may be unfamiliar to many readers. We tend, as already remarked, to see Britain between Victoria's death in 1901 and the outbreak of war in 1914 as a country at the height of imperial power, a nation enjoying stability and peace. In a sense, it was, but only by direct comparison with the slaughter of the trenches on the Western Front and the disruption of the world war which brought that period of British history to an end. Because of this, we have a distorted idea of how the suffragettes fitted into the scheme of things. We often think of them as radicals fighting against the stultifying complacency of a well-ordered and self-satisfied society.

According to this perception, a stubborn and reactionary government refused to take heed of the legitimate demands of disenfranchised women and so they were compelled to take direct action. The reality was that the governments of the day were fighting desperately to preserve peace and order, while simultaneously doing their best to raise the standard of living for average working men and women. They did this while fending off a succession of crises, some of which could have resulted in catastrophe for the country.

From the safe and comfortable perspective of the twenty-first century, the question of women's votes appears to be an absurdly simple one: all that the prime minister of the day had to do was pass a law giving women the vote. In fact, as we have seen, the whole question of extending the parliamentary franchise beyond the limits which had been set by the Reform and Redistribution Acts of 1884–1885 was immensely complicated and no two groups even agreed upon the terms under which it should be undertaken.

The Liberal governments before the First World War found themselves, on more than one occasion, gazing into the abyss, facing the very real prospect of the violent disintegration of the United Kingdom and a state of affairs where the army might end up playing a role in political affairs. In addition to this, these administrations were preparing for the possibility, which became a stark reality in 1914, of a European war. If they were more concerned with tackling such matters and tended as a result to neglect the demands of a few hundred, largely middle-class women, it is possible in retrospect to understand their priorities.

So much for the condition of the nation. What then of the Women's Social and Political Union? What sort of organisation was it and what were those in charge of the WSPU like? The closest parallels to the WSPU that some former members were able to see in later years were found in the fascist movements of Italy and Germany.

It is time now to look closely at the movement which brought forth the suffragettes and to examine in detail what they believed in and how far they were prepared to go for those beliefs.

Chapter Three

An Undemocratic Organisation

The entire class of wealthy women would be enfranchised ... the great body of working women, married or single, would be voteless still.

(Ada Nield Chew, writing of the WSPU in 1904)

On 9 October 1934, the British Union of Fascists, better known as the 'blackshirts', held a rally at the Pier Pavilion in the south coast resort of Worthing. On the platform was the leader of the blackshirts, Sir Oswald Moseley. He was flanked by two of the most important members of the new party. One of these was William Joyce, who would later become famous for broadcasting on behalf of the Germans during the Second World War, during which time he was universally known as 'Lord Haw-Haw'. After the war, Joyce was hanged for treason. The other figure on the stage was a woman. This was Norah Elam, known also as Norah Dacre Fox, and she was perhaps the most influential woman in the British fascist movement. She had also been, from April 1913 until the outbreak of war in the summer of 1914, the General Secretary of the Women's Social and Political Union.

Norah Elam was not the only prominent former suffragette to find her way into the blackshirts. At the same time that she was appearing on a platform alongside Oswald Moseley and Lord Haw-Haw, the chief organiser of the women's section of the British Union of Fascists was Mary Richardson, who had become famous in 1914 for slashing the National Gallery's 'The Rokeby Venus' as a protest against the treatment of Emmeline Pankhurst. The woman who had organised Emily Davison's funeral in 1913, Mary Allen, was also an active member of Moseley's fascists. As well as these well-known suffragettes, there were many former rank and file members of the WSPU to be found in the blackshirt uniform.

It may seem odd to find prominent suffragettes transferring their allegiance to a fascist movement, but it was not really as strange as it might seem. Although many former suffragists drifted left, members of the WSPU, including its founders, tended to move in the opposite direction. Both Emmeline and Christabel Pankhurst became virulently anti-communist after the First World War and Emmeline later stood as a Conservative parliamentary candidate. One of her daughters, Adela, moved even further to the right, to the extent that she was arrested and interned during the Second World War for being a Nazi sympathiser.

Quite apart from politics, there was something about the structure of the Women's Social and Political Union and the way it was run, that seemed to make the British Union of Fascists a logical choice of party in the 1930s for some former members. Even prominent members of the WSPU were aware that Emmeline Pankhurst's commitment to democracy was a little weak. Emmeline Pethick-Lawrence remarked on the paradox that an organisation, 'that was founded upon a desire for the extension of democracy' should have become 'an enthusiastically supported dictatorship'.

In the last two chapters we looked at one or two myths associated with the suffragettes. We must now examine another of these, which is that the Women's Social and Political Union, whose members became known from 1906 onwards as suffragettes, was in some sense a radical, mass movement. Touching closely upon this question is the extent to which the WSPU may be considered in any real meaning of the expression, a democratic organisation or, astonishingly, whether it was really even fighting for democracy. One of the most influential early members of the WSPU, Emmeline Pethick-Lawrence, compared it in retrospect during the 1930s to the fascist movements then in power in Germany, Italy and Spain.

The fact that the WSPU was a tiny group, lacking any wide support among ordinary people, suggests one of the main reasons why they so readily turned to violence in order to get their message across. When a handful of dedicated activists wish to gain the attention of the general public and impose their will upon others, broken windows, burned-out buildings and bomb blasts are potent methods for achieving this. This aspect of the suffragette movement was recognised during the years when they were active, but has become obscured by the passage of time. The idea has developed that the WSPU somehow represented the interests and wishes of ordinary women, that they were the spearhead or vanguard of a popular movement.

This is certainly the version of history often conveyed to children. A popular children's book on the suffragette movement, *Women Win the Vote* (Brian Williams, 2005), says 'On 6 February 1918, women in Britain were awarded the right to vote in general elections for the first time. Many of those women were suffragettes, who had fought a long, hard battle for the right to vote'. Such books take it as given that the Pankhursts and their suffragettes won the right for women to vote in this country. This is done by portraying the WSPU as a mass movement, dedicated to democracy.

Statements such as this, that *many* of the women who were able to vote for the first time in parliamentary elections in 1918 were former suffragettes, are misleading. In fact 8.5 million women were on the electoral register for the 1918 General Election. Yet the membership of the WSPU in 1914 stood at between 3,000 and 5,000; the great majority were nominal members who had simply paid a shilling to join. The hard core of activists probably numbered a thousand at most. Almost all the direct action, the bombings and fire-raising, was carried out or organised by paid workers of the WSPU.

To imagine that the WSPU was in any sense a democratic movement, let alone one with popular support, is quite wrong. The suffragettes were just a small strand in the broader tapestry of the movement for female suffrage. To see them in perspective, one only has to look at the membership figures for the WSPU and compare it with the umbrella group for the moderate suffragists. The National Union of Women's Suffrage Societies, founded in 1897, had, at the outbreak of war in 1914, well over 50,000 members. The WSPU had between 3,000 and 5,000. In other words, for every militant suffragette fighting for the vote by means of violence and disorder, there were at least 10 or 20 moderate suffragists, working peacefully and constitutionally towards the same end.

When the WSPU was founded in 1903, Emmeline Pankhurst was a member of the Independent Labour Party. Her eldest daughter, 23-year-old Christabel, was taking an increasing interest in women's suffrage and it was perhaps this that caused her mother to involve herself again in the question of female emancipation. Sylvia, another daughter, also became a member of the initially small group.

It is ironic to find an organisation campaigning for democracy that is, from the very outset, essentially undemocratic. All previous suffragist groups had both male and female members, but the WSPU forbade men to join from its beginning. The idea of a group formed to fight against discrimination on the grounds of gender instituting such discrimination itself is a fascinating one.

Emmeline and Christabel Pankhurst were also in the habit of falling out with anyone who disagreed with them about either their political aims or the methods by which they chose to work towards those aims. From its very foundation, the WSPU was run by the Pankhursts and they made every decision. Any divergence from their views resulted in members being expelled from the union, so membership entailed not just devotion to a particular ideology, but also personal loyalty to Emmeline and Christabel Pankhurst. The Pankhurts *were* the WSPU.

For the first few years or so of its existence, the WSPU ran in a similar fashion to other suffragist groups. The chief difference between the Women's Social and Political Union and similar groups was that the WSPU was entirely bound up in the personalities and characters of its two founders. Although the Pankhursts remained members of the

Independent Labour Party during this time, there were those in the ILP who regarded them with a good deal of suspicion.

Philip Snowden, who went on to become the Chancellor of the Exchequer in the first Labour government, perceived that to extend the franchise on the terms suggested by the WSPU would mean more votes for the middle and upper classes. Giving women parliamentary votes on the same terms as those that existed for men would serve only to entrench the existing class divisions and do nothing whatever for the benefit of the working classes, either men or women. There were those who believed that the Pankhursts knew this very well and this was the reason why they fought for 'equal' franchise rather than 'universal' franchise. The Pankhursts had no objection to the continued running of the country by the middle and upper classes; they simply wanted women of those social strata to be able to have their share of power alongside well-to-do men. John Bruce Glasier, chairman of the ILP, observed shrewdly of Emmeline and Christabel Pankhurst, 'Really the pair are not seeking democratic freedom but self-importance'.

Quite a few left-wing women, particularly from the working class, also mistrusted the Pankhursts and their demand for 'equal suffrage'. The daughter of a brick maker, Ada Nield Chew, who left school at the age of 11, wrote in 1904 of the idea of 'equal franchise': 'The entire class of wealthy women would be enfranchised ... the great body of working women, married or single, would be voteless still'.

From the point of view of socialists like this, the situation could hardly be simpler. Granting women the vote on the same terms as it was currently given to men would mean giving it to female employers and landowners, while at the same time denying it to those women who worked on their farms or laboured in their sweatshops. It would be an iniquitous move. It has to be said that the Pankhursts' upper-middle-class lifestyle did not exactly endear them to many members of the Labour Party. Glasier said indignantly, when Emmeline Pankhurst was trying to represent herself as a champion of ordinary, working women, 'She has other people's daughters acting as her personal servants'. His wife, Katherine St John, a radical suffragist who had even less time for the pretensions of the WSPU, derided them as being composed almost entirely of upper- and middle-class women. She referred to them as the Society Women's Political Union.

It was this difference of opinion that ultimately caused the Pankhursts not only to leave the ILP themselves, but also to require every member of their organisation to reject any further association with the party. At the Labour Party conference in early 1907, Keir Hardie, the first Labour MP and founder of the Labour Party, put a motion for women's suffrage. This was framed in terms of 'equal' suffrage, in other words, extending the franchise to propertied women on the same terms that men then enjoyed. The conference rejected this and went on to pass by a huge majority a motion calling for universal suffrage, the right to vote in parliamentary elections for every man and woman in the country. Nothing fairer or more democratic could be imagined, but it was enough to cause Emmeline and Christabel Pankhurst to leave the ILP.

The attitude of the WSPU towards democracy can be very clearly seen in their pamphlets, which stated unequivocally that, 'The Women's Social and Political Union are NOT asking for a vote for every woman, but simply that sex shall cease to be a disqualification for the franchise'. This was quite unambiguous. There was no desire to extend the franchise to working men and women. The sole, direct and immediate aim was to ensure that middle-class women who were householders should be able to vote. The WSPU were simply not interested in universal adult suffrage. Indeed, there is reason to suppose that Emmeline Pankhurst was actually opposed to the idea of working-class people being given the vote.

Later in 1907 another incident revealed Emmeline Pankhurst's notion of democracy. The Women's Social and Political Union had a thoroughly democratic constitution, which committed it to annual conferences in which members might vote for changes and select a new committee to run the organisation. A month before the conference was due to be held in October 1907 Emmeline Pankhurst caught wind of the fact that a challenge was planned to the direction in which the WSPU was moving, that is, towards increasing militancy. She regarded this as a personal affront and decided to spike the rebels' guns.

All that those planning to query the running of the WSPU were really wanting was to draw attention to the increasingly autocratic way in which the Pankhursts were behaving. Their aim was to introduce a more democratic approach. These women, who included veteran women's suffrage campaigners, such as 63-year-old Charlotte Despard, wished only to present their case to the annual conference and then accept the result of a vote on their own proposals, as opposed to those made by Emmeline Pankhurst. This attempt to use the democratic process irritated Emmeline and Christabel Pankhurst enormously.

After requesting and receiving pledges of personal loyalty from various important members of the WSPU, Emmeline Pankhurst called an urgent meeting for 10 September, a month before the annual conference. Only members in London were invited to attend this meeting, in the course of which the old constitution was annulled and a list of names for a new committee were read out. All the members of the new committee had been hand-picked for their devotion to Emmeline and Christabel Pankhurst. Before the meeting in September, Emmeline Pankhurst had announced to one of her supporters that she was going to 'tear up the constitution', in order to prevent those with differing views from her own being able to address a large body of WSPU members. As one woman remarked wryly, 'Mrs Pankhurst wants us to have votes, but she does not wish us to have opinions'.

As far as Emmeline Pankhurst was concerned, the situation could hardly have been more clear-cut and simple. She was the leader and her followers should simply obey her orders without question. Little wonder that one of the women ejected from the WSPU after the meeting on 10 September 1907, said that Mrs Pankhurst was behaving like a dictator. In fact, no bones were made about this being precisely what both Emmeline and Christabel Pankhurst wanted – complete control of the members of their organisation. Loyalty towards them should be absolute and unconditional.

The best way to see how Emmeline Pankhurst saw the situation is to read what she herself wrote about the WSPU in *My Own Life*, which was published in 1914:

> *If at any time a member, or a group of members, loses faith in our policy, if any one begins to suggest, that some other policy ought to be substituted, or if she tries to confuse the issue by adding other policies, she ceases at once to be a member. Autocratic? Quite so. But, you may object, a suffrage organisation ought to be democratic. Well the members of the W. S. P. U. do not agree with you. We do not believe in the effectiveness of the ordinary suffrage organisation. The W. S. P. U. is not hampered by a complexity of rules. We have no constitution and by-laws, nothing to be amended or tinkered with or quarrelled over at an annual meeting. In fact, we have no annual meeting, no business sessions, no elections of officers. The W. S. P. U. is simply a suffrage army in the field. It is purely a volunteer army, and no one is obliged to remain in it. Indeed we don't*

want anybody to remain in it who does not ardently believe in the policy of the army.

There is not even the pretence at the organisation being democratic and free admission is made that the WSPU is run in an autocratic fashion. Sylvia Pankhurst, still an ardent socialist, remonstrated with her mother after the attempts to bring democracy to the WSPU: 'Do not fear the democratic constitution. You can carry the conference with you'. It was not a risk that Emmeline Pankhurst and her oldest daughter felt inclined to take.

Nine days after the special meeting in London, a letter sent to all branches of the WSPU explicitly stated that this was not in any way a democratic group: 'We are not playing experiments with representative government. We are not a school for teaching women how to use the vote. We are a militant movement ... It is after all a voluntary militant movement: those who cannot follow the general must drop out of the ranks'. This is quite unambiguous. Members must not expect to influence policy or question the leader, their role is limited to obeying orders.

There were two practical consequences of the events in 1907, one of which was particularly unfortunate. The leadership of the WSPU had always, with one or two exceptions, been thoroughly middle- and upper-class. There were, however, a number of working-class women in the rank and file, particularly in the north of England. Two of the women expelled from the WSPU, Charlotte Despard and Theresa Billington, formed their own group, calling it the Women's Freedom League. Many northern branches of the WSPU went over to the new organisation, leaving the WSPU concentrated in the south of England. The effect was to increase the proportion of middle-class members, making the WSPU even less representative of ordinary working women.

The second effect of the shake-up was that members of the WSPU were required to sign a pledge, stating that they were loyal to the ideals of the WSPU and that they would not support any political party. This of course meant that no members of the Labour Party could remain. It also led to anybody who did not approve of the increasing militancy leaving the WSPU. Those who remained were likely to be middle-class firebrands.

The 1907 purge of what might be termed disloyal elements puts one rather in mind of a revolutionary movement determined to allow no divergent views. Combine this with the cult of personality which almost worshipped the Pankhursts and what emerges is less like a pressure group and more like a cadre of professional revolutionaries. Mrs Pankhurst's followers treated her as an almost superhuman being. After Mary Richardson slashed 'The Rokeby Venus' in the National Gallery with a meat cleaver, she issued a statement saying, 'I have tried to destroy the picture of the most beautiful woman in myth-ological history as a protest against the government for destroying Mrs Pankhurst, who is the most beautiful character in modern history'.

The expulsion from the WSPU of those who disagreed with or even merely questioned the views of Emmeline and Christabel Pankhurst continued. One of their most devoted supporters was Emmeline Pethick-Lawrence who had supported Emmeline Pankhurst during the rebellion in 1907. Five years later, in 1912, Emmeline Pethick-Lawrence and her husband Fred were horrified to learn that the WSPU was going to be taking even more extreme actions than the window-smashing and other vandalism which was already alienating so many potential supporters. They voiced this fear to Emmeline and Christabel, with the result that they too were dropped from the WSPU. Inevitably, the time came when Mrs Pankhurst began to turn against even her own family for their supposed treachery.

Sylvia Pankhurst, one of Emmeline's other daughters, was a socialist and had many dealings with people such as George Lansbury and Keir Hardie. She set up a branch of the WSPU called the East London Federation, which attracted working-class women to the cause of women's suffrage. Sylvia Pankhurst was also in favour of universal adult suffrage, rather than the equal suffrage which had for years been the official policy of the WSPU. This, together with her belief in the practice of democracy in her own organisation, led to her falling out with her mother and sister. This schism was, disturbingly, caused because they felt that she had too strong a belief in democracy. There is a touch of Alice in Wonderland about an organisation such as the WSPU being alarmed about the spread of grass roots democracy.

By 1914, Emmeline and Christabel Pankhurst had had enough of Sylvia's flirtation with democracy. She was summoned to a meeting with them both, a meeting at which her sister did most of the talk-ing, with her mother's approval. Their main objection to Sylvia's activities was plain. Christabel told her, 'You have a democratic con-stitution for your federation, we do not agree with that'. It further emerged that neither Emmeline nor Christabel Pankhurst approved of involving working-class women too much in the suffrage movement. Christabel said that their education was 'too meagre to equip them for the struggle'. She went on, 'Surely it is a mistake to use the weakest for the struggle? We want picked women, the very strongest and most intelligent'.

It is impossible to avoid the feeling that the real objection to what Sylvia Pankhurst was doing was a combination of distrust of democracy and dislike of the working classes being treated as equals. These people needed strong leaders who would tell them what to do, without any of this democratic nonsense. Christabel then said to her sister, 'You have your own ideas. We do not want that, we want all our women to take their instructions and walk in step like an army'.

Interestingly enough, it was when Asquith met a delegation of working women belonging to the East London Federation in 1914 that he apparently began to change his view on women's suffrage. Before that time, he had perhaps seen the suffragettes as middle-class cranks pursuing a fashionable craze. After listening to a group of female industrial workers, who explained their desperate need for the power to vote, Asquith told them that he accepted the logic of their point of view and that, 'If the change has to come, then we must face it boldly and make it thoroughgoing and democratic in its basis'. Some believe that it was simply meeting and listening to these working-class women that helped to bring Asquith around to the view that the franchise should be extended in this way.

When reading what Christabel Pankhurst had to say about working-class people, one senses at best indifference and at worst something approaching contempt. It is interesting to jump ahead of ourselves a little and see how the suffragette activists, who were setting fire to the homes of wealthy and important people as well as planting bombs in public places and damaging the contents of pillar boxes, showed by their actions their own feelings towards the working classes.

It is a curious fact and one which is seldom remarked upon, that the great majority of the victims of suffragette violence were either women or working men who, like the women, did not have the parliamentary vote. To be fair to the suffragettes, this was probably a matter of pragmatism, rather than a conscious desire to harm working-class people. The MPs and Lords with whom the militants of the WSPU really had their quarrel were often too difficult to get close to and so it might have seemed easier to strike at workers than at their bosses or social superiors. Whatever the reason, it was working men and women who bore the brunt of the terrorism.

Supporters of women's suffrage in the Liberal and Labour parties knew at the time that the WSPU were harming innocent people, most of them workers. The suspicion existed that the militants, most of whom belonged to the middle class, were careless about the victims of their attacks. In October 1913, after the bombing campaign had been running in earnest for six months or so, Lloyd George said, 'It's no good burning pavilions, churches and railway sidings and menacing the lives of poor workmen'. At about the same time, the wife of Labour MP Philip Snowden complained that the methods being used by the suffragettes were themselves unjust because they inflicted suffering upon innocent people.

How were the WSPU causing harm to innocent people and, as Lloyd George put it, 'menacing the lives of poor workmen'? To answer this, we will look at the one type of arson which *is* mentioned in modern books on the suffragette movement: the burning and destruction of the contents of letter boxes. This is usually portrayed as a victimless crime, a protest against the 'establishment'.

On 29 November 2012, the Emily Davison Memorial Campaign was launched in London. The aim of this campaign was to persuade those organising the Derby in 2013, on the hundredth anniversary of Davison's death, to hold a minute's silence in her memory. Mention was made at this event of Emily Davison's pioneering role in setting fire to letter boxes. This was described as, 'a bold, brave thing to do' and as 'attacking the establishment'. It might help to make things a little clearer if we look at one or two of the attacks on the postal system initiated by Emily Davison.

On 29 January 1913, a package addressed to Lloyd George burst into flames at a sorting office. There was also a fire in a sorting office in Croydon, while in York glass tubes containing chemicals started a fire when a postman was emptying a pillar box. These fires were caused by phosphorus, fumes from which filled the rooms where the fires broke out. The smoke from burning phosphorus can cause permanent lung damage and the men in the sorting offices were accordingly at risk of suffering serious and irreversible harm to their health. Less than a week later, on 5 February, five postal workers in Dundee were burned, four of them seriously, as they emptied mail bags at a sorting office. A number of letters addressed to Prime Minister Herbert Asquith proved to have in them phosphorous and other chemicals, which reacted when exposed to the air and caused a fire to start. On 22 February, another postman was burned at Lewisham branch post office in south London, when a letter he was handling suddenly caught fire.

Emily Davison's original method for starting fires in letter boxes had proved ineffective. Burning, kerosene-soaked rags tended to die out in the enclosed space of a pillar box as soon as they had used up the available oxygen. More ingenious methods were devised, involving phosphorus and sulphuric acid. These started fires which smouldered and then burst forth when the pillar box was opened or the letters emptied out of the sack in the sorting office and exposed to the air.

On 19 July, six letter box fires took place in Birmingham. A postman clearing one of the boxes had his hand burned severely, because acid had been poured over the letters. In addition to using acids as incendiary agents, the suffragettes had now taken to pouring concentrated sulphuric acid or Spirits of Salts (hydrochloric acid) straight into pillar boxes in order to destroy letters. It was inevitable that some postmen would get these corrosive substances on their hands when they emptied the boxes.

On 22 December 1913, mail bags in Nottingham caught fire and several workers received burns. An incident the following year, on 11 July 1914, not only severely injured a guard on a train, but actually set the train itself on fire while it was travelling from Blackpool to Manchester. A Manchester man called Barlow was sorting letters in a mail van as the train passed through the Lancashire village of Salwick, when one of the mailbags he was handling exploded and caught fire. So fierce were the flames that six other bags of mail also caught fire and the side of the wooden carriage itself then began to burn. Bravely, the guard picked up the burning bags and threw them from the train. He was badly burned on his hands and arms as he did so. He then managed to extinguish the flames, which were threatening to set fire to the train. Later investigations showed that a package in one of the burned mailbags had contained a bottle of sulphuric acid and a quantity of magnesium powder. The bottle had broken and so began the fire.

This is a random sample of the results of the WSPU strategy of targeting pillar boxes and post offices with chemicals such as phosphorus and sulphuric acid. These were really cowardly hit-and-run attacks on working men who, like the suffragettes, did not have the parliamentary vote. The victims were not members of the establishment at all, just ordinary men going about their lives and doing routine and menial jobs. It must have been quite apparent to those putting dangerous chemicals in pillar boxes that they would be very likely to cause harm to the people who handled the packages of phosphorus, or who picked up with their bare hands letters deliberately drenched with sulphuric acid.

In recent years, it has been suggested that many of the wilder actions of the suffragettes were undertaken without the knowledge or approval of the leadership. However, the attacks on postal workers were specifically sanctioned by both Emmeline and Christabel Pankhurst. In December 1913, Mrs Pankhurst reacted angrily on hearing that she was rumoured to disapprove of the campaign against the mail. She said on 5 December, 'Until women get the vote, whether by pillar boxes or other means, women will show their discontent'. In January of the same year, following the defeat of George Lansbury, who resigned his parliamentary seat in order to fight a by-election on the issue of women's suffrage, Christabel Pankhurst wrote in *The Suffragette*: 'By their rejection of the suffrage candidate, the majority of electors ordered women to work out their own political salvation. Those who destroyed the letters acted quickly on this advice. Correspondence would be safe if women had the vote, but if this is denied, they must take the law into their own hands'.

There could be no clearer indication that the leaders of the WSPU endorsed the placing of sulphuric acid and phosphorus in pillar boxes and were therefore ultimately responsible for the attacks in which workers were injured in various ways.

The attacks on postboxes were not isolated or atypical examples of the suffragette strategy. Anybody examining closely the history of the militant campaign might be forgiven for believing that the WSPU saw working-class men and women as unavoidable collateral damage in their struggle.

In the later stages of the suffragette campaign, large country houses owned by politicians who were felt to be unsympathetic to their cause, or even properties owned by the relatives and friends of such people, were burned down by suffragette arson squads. Books written today which mention these attacks almost invariably preface the word 'building' with 'empty', to indicate that the suffragettes would not have harmed anybody. Even in contemporary newspaper reports these houses were typically described as being 'unoccupied'. However, the owners themselves may not have been in residence, but caretakers and domestic staff, many of them women, were invariably living in the servants' quarters. It is little short of a miracle that none of these workers were killed as the result of the arson attacks. Many of the houses were completely destroyed by the fires, which were started with a callous disregard for anybody who was on the premises at the time.

On the night of 4 February 1914, the suffragettes torched Aberuchill Castle in Scotland. The fire swiftly gained a hold and gutted parts of the building. The domestic staff on the upper floors were trapped by the flames and could easily have been killed. Those who started the fire showed complete indifference to the working men and women whose lives were hazarded in this way.

Sometimes, the suffragettes specifically targeted women, with the apparent hope that disrupting their lives or harming their interests would cause them to think hard about the country's political system. It is an unfortunate fact that those affected by such actions were almost invariably working-class women, who would not reap any benefit if the WSPU achieved their goal of 'equal' suffrage. A classic case of this came to light in February 1913 when two members of the WSPU burned down the refreshment pavilion at Kew Gardens.

This was such a senseless act that the proprietor, a Mrs Strange, went to the headquarters of the WSPU to ask why they had done such a thing. She spoke to Harriet Kerr, Secretary of the WSPU. She told Harriet Kerr, 'By burning down the pavilion you did not injure the government but myself and a number of women that I employ'. Kerr responded by saying, 'You take too personal a view of the matter. Your women will, I have no doubt, be very glad by and by to think that they have lent their help'. This conversation was related in court by Mrs Strange after the suffragette leadership was arrested for conspiracy.

With no welfare state to cushion its impact, unemployment in Edwardian Britain could be a serious, even disastrous blow for a working-class family. It did not seem for a moment to have occurred to those activists burning down or blowing up buildings that their actions could be harming people, including even the women whose interests they claimed to be advancing.

Another startling instance of the way in which working-class people were treated as expendable when it came to mounting operations against the supposed enemies of female suffrage, may be seen in the attack on the house that Chancellor of the Exchequer David Lloyd George was having built at Walton-on-the-Hill, near Dorking. Every day, builders, carpenters and plasterers arrived to work on the house at 6.30 am. In the early hours of 19 February 1913, a group of two or three women, including Emily Davison, crept into the almost completed house and planted two bombs, each containing about 5 lbs of explosive.

The fuses for the bombs placed in Lloyd George's new house were primitive in the extreme, consisting of candles placed in saucers full of paraffin-soaked wood shavings. The idea was that as the candle burned down it would set fire to the wood shavings and so ignite a fuse buried among them. It would be very difficult to calculate precisely when a bomb triggered by such an arrangement would detonate. In the event, the first bomb went off with great force at 6.10 am, just 20 minutes before the workmen arrived. It was a close thing and if a workman had arrived a little early that day he could easily have been caught in the blast, which was strong enough to bring down the ceilings, blow out the windows and make a crack in the outer wall of the building which may still be seen today.

The nature of the bomb attack on Lloyd George's house shows that those carrying it out were not overly cautious about the injuries or deaths that could be caused to the men who were employed there. In fact, one of them *was* harmed, although not physically. The explosion destroyed the tools of one of the workmen, and he lost his job as a consequence. A century ago this could easily mean the loss of a man's livelihood, with all that this might entail for his family: hardship, the workhouse or even starvation. It is unlikely that the women who set off these explosions thought for a moment upon the possible consequences of their actions for ordinary men who, like them, had no vote.

One more example should serve to illustrate the indifference towards the livelihoods and, indeed, the very lives of working men and women shown by the suffragettes when conducting their terrorist activities. On the night of 3 April 1913, an empty train standing in a siding at Stockport, a few miles outside Manchester, was attacked by a team of suffragette bombers. They placed firelighters in every carriage, sprinkled paraffin over the seats, and then in one carriage they planted a bomb. Since the train was standing next to a busy railway line, it was perhaps not surprising that when the bomb exploded another train was passing near to it. The force of the blast was great enough to hurl the carriage in which the bomb went off over an embankment. A beam of wood was flung from the destroyed carriage and flew through the cab of the train that was passing. The engine driver could hardly have had a narrower escape. The piece of wood grazed the top of his head, knocking off his cap. An inch lower and he would have been killed.

This incident clearly shows that those carrying out such bombings did not much care who they hurt. Here was an ordinary worker who, under the law as it stood, was not entitled to vote because he was not a householder. Yet those operating on behalf of the WSPU were happy to run the risk of killing such a man, just to make a point. How and why did the WSPU get into the habit of using violence in this way to get across their point? After all, this was not found to be necessary by campaigners for women's suffrage in any other country; it was a purely British phenomenon and limited only to members of the WSPU. The answer is simple and also sheds light upon yet another reason why the WSPU cannot be regarded as a democratic organisation.

The first acts of suffragette militancy were relatively low key. At a speech by Liberal politicians Edward Grey and Winston Churchill in 1905, Christabel Pankhurst and a close friend called Annie Kenney created a disturbance by climbing onto chairs and heckling the speakers. When ushered out by the police, Christabel spat in the face of one and slapped another, for which she and her friend were arrested. This not only brought great publicity to the WSPU, it also caused wealthy donors to send money in support of their aims. Since this small amount of violence and disorder had been so profitable, both financially and in terms of the publicity generated, it was perhaps inevitable that such behaviour should be repeated, on a larger scale and by more women.

Of course, it might have occurred to somebody at this point that since the claim was being made by those who did not want women to be given the parliamentary vote that women were unfit to take part in political activity because they were too emotional and prone to hysteria, then standing on chairs and screaming, spitting, slapping, throwing things and breaking windows were not the best means of disproving such assertions.

The violence increased inexorably over the next few years. Each increase in militant actions resulted in greater publicity and inspired more wealthy backers to come forward. Conversely, any diminution in violence meant a slump in income. The only year that the WSPU saw a drop in contributions was during the time that they eschewed violence during a truce which they called. It must have been obvious that abandoning militant tactics would cause their wealthy backers to withhold their financial help.

Of course, once the WSPU had found such a winning strategy, they had no motive for abandoning it. From breaking windows, the suffragettes moved to starting fires and then causing explosions. They may have been reaping the benefits of increased income and wider publicity from these tactics, but as the violence became more extreme, so the membership of the organisation declined. At the same time, the larger suffragist groups were growing rapidly. This meant that one of the smaller groups was being treated as though it was of greater importance, purely because it was the most aggressive and likely to engage in dangerous activity.

Other democratic groups at this time, such as trade unions and socialist parties, relied for their income upon regular, small contributions from ordinary members. This helped to ensure that they remained genuinely democratic. When the rank and file are paying, they expect to exercise some control over the party or union. This was not the case with the Women's Social and Political Union. They were being subsidised by wealthy people in Kensington and Chelsea, who handed over their money to the leaders of the suffragettes. Since the WSPU refused after the first few years to hold Annual General Meetings, this meant that they could spend the money more or less how they pleased.

The amount of money coming into the Women's Social and Political Union from rich donors is quite simply staggering. Cash receipts for the year 1913/1914 totalled £46,875. This approximates in modern terms to perhaps £3,750,000. Of that enormous sum, less than £50 came from the fees paid by new members. A number of donors were giving over £1,000 a year to the organisation and the only people who decided what this money should be used for were Emmeline and Christabel Pankhurst.

For comparison, the average wage at that time was a little over £1 a week, although many women earned much less than this, perhaps 15s (75p) a week. The WSPU funds enabled the Pankhursts and their close friends in the organisation to give up work and live on the donations pouring in from rich sponsors. After escaping arrest in 1912 and going on the run abroad, Christabel Pankhurst spent two and a half years in Paris, living on this money. Friends of hers were paid £3 or

£4 a week as full-time workers for the suffragette cause. For some idea of what this means, Annie Kenney, a particular favourite of both Pankhursts and for a time acting leader of the WSPU, was being paid four guineas a week. This was a little over four times the average salary at that time. If we take the average salary in the UK today to be around £27,000 a year and then multiply that by four, this might put Annie Kenney's salary at around £110,000 a year today.

Because the Pankhursts were in complete control of the WSPU – ejecting anybody who disagreed with them or even asked too many questions – they were able to use the huge sums of money flowing into the organisation without reference to anybody else. They were accountable to nobody and there is every reason to suppose that their own finances were inextricably tangled up with those of the WSPU. To put it crudely, they and their associates were on to a good thing and were able to live comfortably without the need for conventional jobs.

All the talk by Emmeline and Christabel Pankhurst about the need for followers to obey strong leaders, walking in step and avoiding democracy, as well as the giving of unconditional allegiance and adulation to one person – a recurring theme in the suffragette move-ment – might bring to mind other extremist political movements which became popular in certain European countries during the 1930s. In this connection, it is curious to reflect that WSPU rallies were some-times spectacular affairs, with everybody decked out in the white, green and purple colours of the organisation – white chosen for purity, green for hope and purple for majesty. Banners often featured pictures of Mrs Pankhurst and many of those attending wore badges showing a portrait of Emmeline Pankhurst. It does not take much imagination to see these adoring crowds come to see their beloved leader as pre-cursors of the Nuremburg rallies. Certainly, such a political cult of personality had never been seen before in the United Kingdom.

A number of former suffragettes noticed this resemblance in later years. Cicely Hamilton, who had worked energetically for the cause of female suffrage, described Emmeline Pankhurst as 'a forerunner of Lenin, Hitler and Mussolini – the leader who could do no wrong'. An examination of the subsequent stories of some of those who were important figures in the WSPU is revealing when viewed from this perspective.

The almost mindless way in which her followers accepted any position taken by Emmeline Pankhurst was neatly illustrated on the outbreak of war in 1914. So conditioned had members of the WSPU become to blindly obey the whims of Emmeline and Christabel Pankhurst that many would adopt any position that they were instructed to take. Even so, it came as a surprise to them when Mrs Pankhurst told them that they must now drop their campaign and throw all their weight behind Prime Minister Herbert Asquith. After being told for six years that he was practically the devil incarnate, they were now to follow him as a wise and benevolent national leader.

Emmeline Pankhurst dropped the fight for women's suffrage as readily as she had previously abandoned socialism. Instead, she became ferociously patriotic and encouraged men to join the army to fight Germany. Later on, she became an opponent of strikes and offered her help in breaking the General Strike of 1926. She was finally adopted as a parliamentary candidate for the Conservative Party. As she threw herself into each new craze, so Mrs Pankhurst seemed to lose interest in the previous one. During the war, she was consulted by Lloyd George on the matter of women's suffrage and she told him to make whatever arrangements he felt necessary. She was no longer in the least concerned about the notion of equal suffrage, the cause which had resulted in such bitter disputes with her colleagues, friends and family. In the event, the bill that brought some women the vote in 1918 did not incorporate either universal or equal suffrage – men could vote at 21 years of age, some women at 30. By then, Emmeline Pankhurst was visiting Russia and America as part of her crusade against Bolshevism, her latest interest.

Other prominent suffragettes, including all three of her daughters, also turned to other causes. Christabel found religion and devoted her life to working for the Seventh Day Adventists, an evangelical Christian denomination. Sylvia became involved with the mystical sect of Theosophy and the youngest daughter, Adela, after moving through the whole spectrum of political belief, settled down as a sympathiser of the Nazi regime in Germany. During the Second World War, she was interned in Australia as a possible fifth columnist, due to her admiration for the Third Reich. Curiously enough, she was not alone in this among former suffragettes. What possible connection could there be between the suffragettes and the fascists? Some former activists saw distinct similarities.

In the late 1930s, Emmeline Pethick-Lawrence, once a close associate of the Pankhursts but later expelled by them from the WSPU, observed uneasily the similarities between the suffragettes and the fascist movements in Italy and Germany. Writing in 1938, she said, 'It is so-called upholders of democracy who create, when they are false in their principles, and when they attempt to crush their opponents, dictatorships'. She also remarked that the WSPU 'bore a certain resemblance to the dictatorships so common in the world today'. Writing in the 1930s, Cecily Hamilton, another former suffragette, said that the WSPU was 'the first indication of the dictatorship movements which are by way of thrusting democracy out of the European continent'.

WSPU members often seemed to find that the demise of the union left a gap in their lives. Some filled this gap by becoming writers and artists; others became involved in various churches or political movements, including both socialism and the fight against vivisection. For some of the most high-profile campaigners, the political landscape between the wars contained a very attractive new ideology, a political philosophy which they felt embodied many of the features which they had found so congenial in the WSPU.

Mary Richardson, who had hacked at the Velasquez masterpiece in the National Gallery, was drawn to the British fascist movement under Oswald Mosley. Richardson had been in the thick of much of the suffragette action in the years leading up to the First World War. She went on to become the chief organiser of the British Union of Fascists women's section and saw in retrospect the suffragettes as a proto-fascist movement. She wrote:

I was first attracted to the Blackshirts because I saw in them the courage, the action, the loyalty, the gift of service, and the ability to serve which I had known in the suffragette movement. When later I discovered that Blackshirts were attacked for no visible cause or reason, I admired them the more when they hit back and hit back hard.

For this leading suffragette at least, the blackshirts were in some way the natural successor to the Women's Social and Political Union.

Norah Elam, also known as Mrs Dacre Fox, was once the General Secretary of the WSPU. Like Mary Richardson, she was imprisoned for her suffragette activities, going on hunger strike on three occasions. Elam and her husband joined the British Union of Fascists soon after it was formed and she became a prominent figure in its women's section, writing many articles in praise of fascism as an ideology. She stood as a parliamentary candidate for Northampton. In 1940, she and her husband were both arrested and interned under Defence Regulation 18b as possible fifth columnists. Like Mary Richardson, she saw in the structure of the WSPU a forerunner of the fascist movement. She wrote during the 1930s:

> *The Women's Movement, like the Fascist Movement, was conducted under strict discipline, and cut across all party allegiances: its supporters were drawn from every class and party. It appealed to women to forget self-interest: to relinquish petty personal advantage, the privilege of the sheltered few for the benefit of the many: and to stand together against the wrongs and injustices which were inherent in a system so disastrous to the well-being of the race. Like the Fascist movement, too, it chose its Leader, and once having chosen gave that leader absolute authority to direct policy and destiny, displaying a loyalty and devotion never surpassed in the history of this country.*

She even described Sir Oswald Mosley as a 'latter day Mrs Pankhurst'. Elam, it must be remembered, was no rank and file member of the WSPU but its General Secretary, one of the first suffragettes ever to undergo force-feeding.

Another of her quotations, from the 22 February 1935 edition of *The Blackshirt*, gives us a lucid description of the feelings of this former, high-ranking member of the WSPU:

> *No woman who loves her country, her sex or her liberty, need fear the coming victory of Fascism. Rather, she will find what the suffragettes dreamt about twenty odd years ago is now becoming a possibility, and woman will buckle on her armour for the last phase of the greatest struggle, for the liberation of the human race, which the world has yet seen.*

Stirring stuff indeed and a good indication of the way in which the ideology of the suffragette movement could dovetail neatly with that of Mosley's blackshirts.

Another prominent member of the WSPU who became enamoured of fascism in the 1930s was Mary Sophia Allen. Allen was the WSPU's organiser for south-west England and was imprisoned three times for breaking windows. An early hunger striker, she was force-fed on one occasion. It was Mary Allen who organised Emily Davison's spectacular funeral procession through central London. Like many in the WSPU, including of course Emmeline Pankhurst herself, Mary Allen was bitterly opposed to communism, which she saw as the major threat to the world. Her anxieties about a Bolshevik takeover in this country led to her meeting Hitler, Franco and Mussolini during the thirties.

When the Second World War began in 1939, consideration was given to imprisoning Allen under the Defence of the Realm Act, but in the end, this was not thought to be necessary. Instead, she was subjected to an order which prevented her from travelling more than five miles from her home and forbade her to use a telephone or radio. It was feared that she might, in fact, be a spy for the Nazis.

The need to follow a strong leader, to whom unconditional obedience is pledged; the belief that the great mass of ordinary people are not able to decide for themselves what they need; the camaraderie of being a part of a group which is in opposition to the established order – all these were features that might have made the blackshirts attractive to the same type of women who had previously gravitated to the suffragette movement. The obsession with the health of the 'race', which both Emmeline and Christabel vigorously espoused, also fitted neatly into this picture.

Another aspect of the British Union of Fascists worth noting is that between a fifth and a quarter of the members were women. This was a far higher proportion than any of the other parties in existence at that time boasted. Moseley acknowledged his debt to the female members of his movement, writing: 'My movement has largely been built by the fanaticism of women; they hold ideals with tremendous passion. Without women, I could not have got a quarter of the way'.

Of course, not all members of the WSPU were secretly fascist sympathisers, but there were enough similarities between the suffragettes and the fascists to raise more than a few eyebrows. The jingoistic patriotism displayed by Emmeline and Christabel Pankhurst during the First World War, the fanatical distrust not only of communists, but any working man who went on strike, the uncritical adoration of a strong leader, the uniforms and spectacles of public rallies, the readiness to use violent means to achieve political ends – all of these were common both to the WSPU and later fascist movements in Italy, Germany and also in this country.

Some of the similarities between the WSPU and the British Union of Fascists were uncanny. In May 1909, the WSPU organised a 'Women's Exhibition', which was held at the old ice skating rink in Knightsbridge. The building was covered in green, white and purple banners and once inside, it was clear that this was not just another bazaar of the kind beloved of middle-class women. For one thing, there were demonstrations of ju-jitsu, an unarmed combat technique, which some of the suffragettes employed when fighting with the police or those intent on disrupting their meetings. There was the world's first all-female drum and fife marching band, which played rousing tunes. Even stranger were the displays of drill, with women marching and standing to attention under the supervision of drill instructors. Among the souvenirs on offer were dolls dressed as suffragettes in the colours of the WSPU.

Thirty years later, women in the British Union of Fascists, including a number of former suffragettes, were involved in identical activities, learning ju-jitsu, drilling in military fashion, selling dolls dressed as blackshirts and following a charismatic leader who required unconditional personal devotion.

Far from being a mass movement, the WSPU was a small group of activists who felt that they knew better than ordinary people what was good for them. When those ordinary people showed no enthusiasm for what was being suggested, a hard core of militants attempted to force agreement by the use of violence. The bombings and arson attack were carried out in the main by paid workers from the WSPU and sanctioned by the leadership of the organisation, Mrs Pankhurst specifically endorsing both bomb attacks and fire-raising.

The WSPU did not engage in terrorism from the beginning, although there is reason to suppose that the possibility of such activity was considered soon after its founding. The suffragettes began with fairly mild disorder and violence and moved, step by step, towards out-and-out terrorism when they realised that constitutional methods were proving too slow for them.

Chapter Four

The Use of Terror and the Need for Martyrs

❝ The prominence that would be given to this in the press would probably act on the minds of these half-insane women, and might suggest ... the very act it was hoped to avoid. ❞

(Police report on a suspected suffragette plot to assassinate Prime Minister Asquith, 1909)

It is quite impossible at this late stage to discover whether or not the Pankhursts planned from the beginning that members of their organisation would set fire to buildings and plant bombs. It is curious, however, that Emmeline Pankhurst chose for what she described as the WSPU's 'permanent motto', the slogan, 'Deeds, not words'.

The idea of attracting attention to a political cause through violent acts, such as assassinations and bombings, was not a new one when the WSPU began and had by that time become known as 'Propaganda by the deed', which sounds very similar to Mrs Pankhurst's 'Deeds not words'. Some nineteenth century revolutionaries had concluded that writing long and convoluted tracts of political philosophy was not an effective way of getting their message across. They decided that the explosion of a bomb or violent death of a politician would catch the attention of the general public far more rapidly than mere words alone; it was a statement that could not be ignored. This was 'Propaganda by the deed'; deeds, rather than words being used to get the point across. Not only could bombings be used to publicise a cause in this way, they could also be part of a deliberate strategy to force political change. It is in the light of this tradition that Emmeline Pankhurst's choice of the expression, 'Deeds, not words', must be interpreted.

It is sometimes forgotten that Britain had a history of terrorism in the latter part of Victoria's reign. There is often a tendency today to view terrorism as being a modern phenomenon, a scourge of the late twentieth century and the early twenty-first century, but that is very far from being the case. The worst loss of life in a terrorist attack in London before the 7/7 tube bombings in 2005, for instance, was caused by the detonation of a quarter of a ton of gunpowder placed outside London's Clerkenwell House of Detention in 1867. Twelve people were killed in this explosion, which demolished a row of houses and caused damage to windows and chimney pots half a mile away.

The Clerkenwell Outrage, as it became known, was Victorian England's 9/11. Troops were mobilised and police officers armed in the aftermath of this terrible event. The suspicion was that the explosion in Clerkenwell was to be the first in a series of attacks by Irish terrorists which might be aimed at destroying landmarks from the Houses of Parliament to St Paul's Cathedral. There was talk of introducing identity cards and enlisting concerned citizens in a new militia to guard the capital against further outrages. The man who lit the fuse for this bomb, an Irishman called Michael Barrett, found fame of a sort as the last man in this country to be hanged in public. His name lives on to this day. 'Mick Barrett' became a pejorative term for Irishmen, which lingers on as 'Micks'.

A few years after the Clerkenwell Outrage, Irish extremists conducted a more systematic bombing campaign in England, using dynamite to attack Scotland Yard, the Tower of London, parliament and the London Underground. Visitors to museums and other tourist attractions now had to wait in line to have their bags searched and precautions were taken to protect bridges and public buildings with security grilles to prevent bombs being placed near them. There were some who mocked, but on 13 December 1884, these measures paid off. On that Saturday night, three men in a rowing boat tried to attach a large device containing nitroglycerine to the underside of London Bridge. The newly installed grilles there frustrated their efforts and caused the bomb to be mishandled. The resulting explosion did little harm to London Bridge, but killed all three of the bombers. Paddington Station was targeted on 30 October 1883 and on that same day the first tube bombing in London's history took place near Charing Cross Station. On 20 January 1885, another bomb exploded on the underground, this time at Gower Street Station.

The Irish were not the only people planting bombs in Victorian London. In 1894 a bomb exploded near Greenwich Observatory and three years later came the first death in a tube bombing, when a charge of dynamite went off on a train at Aldersgate Station, which has since been renamed Barbican. These attacks were the work of anarchists.

The fear of terrorism was keen in Edwardian Britain, although focused less on domestic terrorists than on gunmen and bombers who might be hiding among the hundreds of thousands of asylum seekers flooding into the country. In January, 1909, an unarmed police officer was shot dead in Tottenham during a bungled robbery by eastern European asylum seekers, who had been raising funds for a terrorist group. Two years later, on 16 December 1910, five police officers were gunned down, three of whom died of their wounds. The killers were members of a gang of foreign terrorists. These murders culminated in the so-called 'Siege of Sydney Street', in London's East End. The army were called in to deal with the gunmen.

In the Edwardian period, as now, the various subversive movements with terrorist leanings often crossed paths and shared information and resources. In recent years, we have seen connections of this sort between, for instance, the IRA and the PLO. Much the same happened in the years leading up to the First World War. One such association saw some suffragettes moving in the same circles which had seen a political murder being committed, the first in this country for many decades. Although most of those harmed by the suffragettes' attacks were working people, there were a number of plots to kill politicians and even the occasional magistrate. It has only recently been revealed that there were also plans to assassinate the Prime Minister himself in 1909.

One of the lesser-known terrorist groups operating in Britain during Edward VII's reign was based at a large house in Highgate, the headquarters of the Indian Home Rule Society. The house was used by Indians opposed to British rule in their country. Various illegal activities took place there, ranging from bomb-making to gunrunning. The activists, many of them students who lived at the so-called 'India House', practised marksmanship at a shooting gallery a stone's throw from the British Museum. The name of this range was, improbably enough, 'Fairyland' and it was situated at 92 Tottenham Court Road (see Plate 3).

Some of those frequenting the shooting gallery in Tottenham Court Road used the rifles and pistols supplied there, others brought their own weapons. Young men from the Indian Home Rule Society often arrived there to practise shooting with very modern Browning, semi-automatic pistols. One of the Indians, Madan Lal Dhingra, who had close contact with India House was a 22-year-old engineering student at University College London. On 1 July 1909, he put the skills he had acquired to good effect when he carried out the first political assassination seen in London for a hundred years.

On the evening of 1 July, the Secretary of State for India, Lord Morley, was due to attend a public meeting at the Institute for Imperial Studies in London. Instead, he sent his political aide-de-camp, Sir Curzon Wyllie. As Wyllie entered the hall, Madan Lal Dhingra approached and shot him in the face four times, killing him on the spot. The Indian was seized by members of the audience and less than three weeks later found himself in the dock at the Old Bailey on trial for his life.

One of those who gave evidence at the trial was the proprietor of the Tottenham Court Road shooting gallery. He testified that the defendant was known to him and had been in the habit of bringing an automatic pistol to his range and practising his shooting. On the evening of 1 July, at about 5.30 pm, only two hours before the assassination, Madan Lal Dhingra had arrived at his range with an automatic pistol and fired 12 shots at a target, from a distance of 18 feet. The target was produced for the jury and it was seen that 11 of the shots had hit it. The gun used in that session, a Belgian Browning automatic, was the same one used to kill Sir Curzon Wyllie.

Madan Lal Dhingra was sentenced to death and hanged on 17 August. Scotland Yard's Special Branch began to investigate both the India House and also the shooting gallery which had been at the centre of the assassination. They soon learned something very alarming – Indian nationalists were not the only dissidents learning to shoot in Tottenham Court Road. Henry Morley, owner of Fairyland, told the police that two women had been coming there over the summer to practise shooting. Intriguingly, they brought with them their own pistol, which happened to be a Browning automatic of the same type used in the recent assassination. These were state-of-the-art weapons, much more sophisticated than the revolvers generally in use at that time. By then, the police had already found evidence which suggested that the Indian Home Rule Society had been involved in smuggling crates of such pistols to India, where they were being used by extremists.

In September, there was an even more disturbing development. From July to October 1909, members of the Women's Freedom League, a moderate and non-violent group of suffragists, had been picketing parliament. A member of the organisation contacted the police and claimed that this picket had been infiltrated by women who planned to shoot Prime Minister Herbert Asquith as he left the House. Special Branch officers interviewed the woman who wrote to them about this plot and satisfied themselves that there was cause for concern.

The identities of the women who had been learning to shoot were never revealed. Asquith refused to agree to police requests to ban demonstrators from parliament and the most that could be done was to increase the number of bodyguards assigned to the Prime Minister. There were sound tactical reasons for not clearing away the protesters who were picketing the House of Commons – it could precipitate the very act it was hoped to avoid. As the official police report put it:

The serious matter is that we should have to make known the facts leading us to believe that there is a conspiracy to murder the PM. The prominence that would be given to this in the press would probably act on the minds of these half-insane women, and might suggest effectively

the commission of the very act which we wish to prevent. Moreover, the
removal of the pickets would be looked on by them as an act of violence
and injustice, and would make them furious and more ready to commit
such a crime.

That the two women who were practising shooting at Fairyland were
using exactly the same, exceedingly unusual, pistol as that used to
shoot Sir Curzon Wyllie, caused eyebrows to be raised at Scotland
Yard. That they should be learning to shoot at the same place that
Wyllie's assassin had been frequenting a few weeks earlier was also a
curious coincidence. The men from India House were known for their
links with Irish Fenians and it was entirely possible that they had also
been friendly with suffragette activists. In the event, the women who
had been seen at Fairyland dropped from sight and the ostentatious
new security precautions did the trick: there was no attempt on
Asquith's life.

None of the terrorist actions that took place in Victorian and
Edwardian Britain achieved the end hoped for by those carrying them
out. They certainly attracted publicity, but most people were shocked
at the violence and not moved to sympathise with the aims of the
terrorists in the slightest. It is in this context that the suffragette
bombing campaign must be seen.

England had already experienced terrorism and had shown no
inclination to surrender to it. Either the suffragettes were unaware of
this or perhaps they thought that their own cause was so strong and
morally justified that public reaction would be different. This was a
terrible miscalculation because, although the violence certainly captured more attention for the suffragettes, it also lost them support,
generating instead revulsion for the actions of the extremists and
sympathy for the government which had to tackle such a problem. In
short, suffragette terrorism produced precisely the opposite effect
from that which was intended. This is always a danger for those using
terrorism as a political weapon. It is difficult to judge in advance
whether your cause will be advanced or irrevocably harmed by the
starting of fires and the causing of explosions.

Why did the WSPU think that the bombs they were planting might
help their campaign? There are several ways that terrorism can be
used to achieve political ends. One way is as part of a strategy to pro-
voke a general uprising against a repressive government. This entails
the systematic use of violence to such a degree that the state responds

with harsh measures, typically deploying soldiers and torturing or executing those who oppose the status quo. Once this repression gets under way, the general population becomes caught up in the situation, suffering from the tactics used by the government and its agents. They are then driven into the arms of the revolutionaries and so realise that they have a common interest in the overthrow of the regime. It is hardly necessary to remark that this particular plan would have had little chance of success in Britain at that time.

There is a second way that terrorism may be used by a small and undemocratic group to get what it wants, a method that is more suited to a democratic society. If you can make enough of a nuisance of yourself and cause sufficient disruption to the lives of ordinary people, then there might come a point at which the mood of the public is in favour of the government making concessions or even giving in entirely to those creating the annoyance, just so that ordinary, peaceful life may resume.

After Herbert Asquith replaced Campbell-Bannerman as Prime Minister in 1908, the WSPU began to become more aggressive. From shouting slogans, they moved to smashing windows and chaining themselves to railings. This is all nuisance and vandalism, rather than terrorism. We can precisely date the onset of straightforward terrorism by the suffragettes. It began on the evening of 18 July 1912.

Perhaps the best way to decide if the four women whose actions resulted in their appearing in court in Dublin that year really *were* terrorists is to look at the charges which they faced. Here are some of the 12 charges that were read out by the clerk of the court before their trial:

Having on July 18th last feloniously, unlawfully and maliciously set fire to the Theatre Royal, unlawfully causing an explosion in the theatre by means of a metal case containing an explosive in the nature of gunpowder, causing by means of gunpowder an explosion of a nature likely to cause serious injury to property, causing by means of a certain explosive unknown an explosion of a nature likely to endanger life and conspiring with other persons to cause an explosion in the United Kingdom likely to endanger life.

It is hard to imagine reading in tomorrow's newspaper about people being charged with such offences and not assuming that this was a possible terrorist conspiracy. Still, perhaps it was all nonsense and the police had exaggerated what these four women had been up to? Actually, there was no argument about the events which led to the trial in Dublin that year. The suffragette newspaper *Votes for Women* agreed that the actions of which they were accused had actually taken place. The only debate was whether or not those actions were justifiable.

In July 1912, Prime Minister Herbert Asquith visited Dublin in the company of the Irish nationalist MP John Redmond. On 18 July, he and Redmond, accompanied by the Lord Mayor of Dublin, rode through the city in an open carriage to general acclaim. This was a triumphal procession to draw attention to the Home Rule Bill, which would accord Ireland a degree of autonomy. As they passed cheering crowds, a woman darted out and threw a hatchet at Asquith's face. It missed him, but sliced through John Redmond's cheek and ear. Wrapped around the haft of the small axe was a piece of paper bearing the words, 'This symbol of the extinction of the Liberal Party for ever-more'.

The following day, Asquith was due to make a speech at the Theatre Royal. On the evening of the 18 July, a variety show was held at the theatre, with an orchestra and various performers. The place was full and as the audience was about to leave, three women began trying to burn the theatre down. They poured petrol on carpets and curtains, setting fire to them. One of the women, seated in a box, managed to set fire to a chair, which she then hurled down at the orchestra. As if this was not dangerous enough, several bombs were also detonated and an attempt was made to start a fire in the cinema projector room, where reels of highly inflammable film were stored.

Witnesses describe scenes of pandemonium, with flames leaping up the curtain surrounding one box and the theatre filling with smoke after an explosion which, according to a soldier who was present, sounded like artillery fire. The situation in the theatre was unbelievably dangerous. John Moody, conductor of the Theatre Royal orchestra, sub-sequently gave evidence as to what he saw. A woman threw a blazing chair from the box above the orchestra pit and the chair struck the wall, then landed near to the cello player. He watched as the woman who had thrown the chair set fire to the curtains on the box nearest the stage. They immediately began to blaze. He also saw the fire in the projector room and heard an explosion, which filled the theatre with smoke. Four women were seized by outraged theatre goers and later charged with a series of offences, including conspiracy to commit grievous bodily harm, in connection with the attack on the Prime Minister and various other charges relating to the explosions and fire at the theatre.

Perhaps we should pause at this point and consider these actions. Throwing a hatchet at somebody's head is almost certain to result in serious injury – you would be lucky not to blind or disfigure your victim by such an action; you could even kill somebody in that way. That only a few cuts and grazes were inflicted upon one of the men in the carriage was merely good fortune; the intention was surely to maim or disfigure the man at whom the weapon was hurled.

Starting a fire and then setting off explosions in a crowded theatre is foolhardy and dangerous. Quite apart from the obvious risk of burning the building down with the possible loss of life, there is also the risk of causing a panic and stampede for the exits, in which people could be crushed to death. Anybody splashing petrol around, setting it on fire and then detonating bombs in a theatre full of people must be at the very least expecting to cause injury or death.

Who were the women who carried out these attacks? Were they lunatics on the fringe of the suffragette movement, extremists who were operating more or less on their own initiative? In fact, all were at the very heart of the movement, and long-standing members of the WSPU. There is a general tendency to play down dangerous or outlandish actions by suffragettes and pretend that those carrying them out were acting against the wishes of the leadership. Emily Davison is sometimes described, for example, as a 'lone wolf', somebody who acted independently and without the sanction of the WSPU leaders. In the case of those involved in the first indisputable terrorist action by suffragettes, such a defence is not possible.

One of the women arrested and subsequently convicted for her part in the attack on the Theatre Royal was 45-year-old Sarah Jane Baines, more commonly known as Jennie Baines. In April 1908, Baines had been appointed full-time organiser for the WSPU in the Midlands and North of England. She received for this work a wage of £2 a week. Mabel Capper, although acquitted of causing any damage, was also an organiser for the WSPU in Manchester. Gladys Evans had been a member of the WSPU marching band and was also a paid employee of the WSPU.

Mary Leigh was a Drum Major in the same marching band and was being paid a salary of over a £1 a week, a decent wage at that time. She was a close friend of Emily Davison and had carried out a number of actions in the company of other WSPU organisers. Three years before the attempt to burn down the theatre in Dublin, she had been involved in an attack during a visit to Birmingham by Asquith. Her protests then were, like the attack in Dublin, carried out together with paid WSPU organisers. The Birmingham protest too was a violent one, in the course of which a police officer was badly injured and several passers-by also needed medical attention.

Emmeline Pankhurst had already said, by the time of the attempt to burn down the Theatre Royal, that she would never disown the actions of any members of the WSPU which were undertaken in the further-ance of its aims. This could be (and indeed at the Old Bailey the following year it was) taken as encouragement and incitement of violence. Having already openly urged the smashing of windows and other destruction of property, Mrs Pankhurst did not hesitate a few months later to endorse even the bombing of a cabinet minister's home. Those who carried out the attack on the theatre in Dublin were not disowned by the WSPU; in fact, when the police raided the London headquarters of the WSPU the following spring, two of the women on the premises at the time had been among those charged with the arson and bombing of the Theatre Royal.

Five days before the attack in Dublin, a serious attempt to set fire to the home of Lewis Harcourt, Secretary of State for the Colonies was thwarted by the vigilance of a police constable in Oxfordshire. In the early hours of 13 July, PC Godden apprehended a woman loitering near the grounds of Nuneham House, Harcourt's country residence. She was carrying a satchel which contained cans of oil, boxes of matches, wax tapers, fire lighters and various other incriminating materials. Also found was a statement, which explained the actions the woman was about to take.

Helen Craggs, the woman arrested that night, had since 1910 been a paid organiser of the WSPU. She was, like the others who were carry-ing out the arson and bombing attacks, close to the leadership of the organisation. This involvement was exceedingly deep – Helen Craggs was romantically entangled with Emmeline Pankhurst's son Harry. It is inconceivable that Mrs Pankhurst should not have been aware that this woman was proposing to burn down a cabinet minister's house.

The leadership of the WSPU were evidently pursuing two simul-taneous strategies when it came to the use of bombing and arson. We shall see later how these different strands ran alongside each other as the campaign gathered momentum throughout 1913 and 1914. On the one hand there were the targeted attacks on members of the government and others whom the suffragettes felt were enemies of their cause. There were also actions aimed at the general public, particularly men. This too is a classic tactic of terrorism, as outlined by ideologues of the late nineteenth century. So closely does the terrorist campaign conducted by leading members of the WSPU follow the pattern outlined in writings by revolutionaries in Britain, Russia and America, that it is all but impossible to view their actions as random attacks undertaken without a coherent, underlying plan. This was not a collection of scattered, spur of the moment outrages carried out by sympathisers, it was a methodical and systematic crusade directed by a determined leadership.

The decision to resort to bombings in public places was almost certainly a deliberate and calculated move by the WSPU, once they saw that attacks limited to the government and its agents were proving ineffective in rousing the public and persuading them to support the suffragettes. There were, at least at the beginning of the terrorism, sound historical reasons for favouring such a strategy.

When attacks are limited to agents of the government and property owned by the government, then many people soon become a little blasé about such incidents. It begins to look like a private quarrel between the leaders of the country and a group of people who are opposed to them. After all, the windows broken by the suffragettes in government offices did not really affect anybody other than the civil service clerks working there. Finding that your local church has been burned to the ground though, brings it home that you are not merely a bystander to this dispute, it can also have a direct and unpleasant effect upon you. When this happens, perhaps you yourself will start urging the government to give these people what they want, just to end the nuisance that is being caused to you, regardless of how sensible the aims of the terrorists are.

This strategy can be expanded in various ways so that other organisations will, reluctantly, end up supporting your cause and urging the government to settle. This sort of unwilling support for the aims of a terrorist group was exploited by the WSPU and took the form of economic terrorism, amounting, in effect, to something like a protection racket. The main aim of lighting fires and setting off explosives was not to harm people, although the suffragettes were certainly quite careless about this on many occasions. The most significant purpose was simply to create publicity. Another was to drain the resources of insurance companies and small businesses and so cause them to beg the government to take steps to end the attacks. The accounts of some of the fires started in 1913, the estimates of the financial costs incurred are pretty breathtaking.

Two fairly typical examples are the destruction by fire of St Catherine's Church in Hatcham on 6 May 1913 and the bombing of the Britannia Pier in Yarmouth on 17 April 1914. The suffragettes had a bit of a bee in their bonnet about churches, which they viewed as being complicit in the patriarchal society which was denying them votes. A number were blown up or torched as a result. The rebuilding of St Catherine's Church in 1913 was estimated to cost £20,000 (roughly equating today to about £1,600,000). The damage to the pier at Yarmouth, which was caused by a bomb, was quoted by the owner as being in the region of £15,000 (something over £1,200,000 today).

These two instances are not at all exceptional. They pale into insignificance when compared with the initial estimates for the loss of buildings and property at the great Portsmouth Dockyard fire in December 1913, which was commonly regarded as the work of the suffragettes. The cost of rebuilding was announced by the navy to be about £200,000.

These were colossal sums for the insurance companies to find and the WSPU made no bones about their intention to drive some businesses to bankruptcy by their tactics. This began with the mass destruction of plate-glass shop windows in 1912. Some of these shops had insurance, for others, the cost of replacing their windows would have to be borne by their own business. This sort of thing was a win-win situation for the suffragettes. Property insurance was not nearly as common a century ago as it is now, even for commercial premises. Either a small business would find itself with a huge bill for new windows, for example, which it might not be able to pay, or an insurance company would find its profits cut by the amount that was being paid out for attacks.

It was suggested by some leading suffragettes that the big insurance companies began to support votes for women at about this time because they could see their profit margins dwindling. It was said that they were anxious for the government to give in to the militancy, just so that they would stop having to pay out such large sums each month. And the sums really were very large. In February 1914 alone, for instance, the cost of the damages caused by suffragette arson attacks was estimated to be £62,000. It would have been a great relief for the companies paying out such vast sums if the suffragette campaign could be brought to a halt. The easiest way of doing that would be for the government to give in to their demands.

It is for the reasons outlined above that we read of the burning of woodyards and haystacks by suffragettes, as well as the larger fires which destroyed churches and stately homes. All such attacks inconvenienced somebody, all had ultimately to be paid for from somebody's pocket.

Hand in hand with the use of terrorism went the quest for the raising up of martyrs, as is so often the case with terrorist campaigns. A few martyrs can turn around the fortunes of a militant group and restore their popularity if it appears to be waning. These martyrs should ideally be killed by the state, either by being formally executed or just shot down in the streets. An example of this took place in 1916 with the Easter Rising in Dublin. This involved just over 1,000 Republicans seizing control of key parts of the city from the British. Those who undertook this adventure were extremely unpopular with the citizens of Dublin. In one incident, the Sinn Féin rebels actually opened fire on Dublin citizens who were shouting abuse and trying to disarm them. After they had been captured by the British army, the rebels were booed, jeered and spat at by angry crowds of Dubliners. The soldiers escorting the captured rebels were forced to protect them from the mobs.

Everything changed within a few weeks. The British executed 15 of the leaders of the rising and these men instantly became martyrs. Their execution was instrumental in changing the attitude of the public to the cause for which they had died. Had the leaders of the revolt simply been sent to prison, the Easter Rising might not hold the iconic place it does in the hearts of many Irish men and women today.

The WSPU recognised the need for martyrs fairly early in their militant campaign. Governments though are often only too aware of the dangers in allowing their opponents to become martyrs and sometimes take great steps to prevent this happening. The WSPU must have known very well that there was not the slightest chance of the government obliging them by killing any suffragettes. If they wanted martyrs, then they would have to manufacture them for themselves, without the assistance of Asquith's government. This would prove a tricky but not insurmountable problem.

Asquith was a canny enough operator to be fully conscious of the risk of martyring any members of the WSPU. There was little chance of his government going as far as hanging or shooting anybody for breaking windows or even starting fires, but the suffragettes hit upon another tactic which they felt might provide them with the necessary symbolic death.

In June, 1909, a 44-year-old supporter of the WSPU called Marion Wallace-Dunlop stamped a quotation from the Bill of Rights onto the side of St Stephen's Hall at the House of Commons. She used indelible ink which, according to the charge made after her arrest, caused damage to the value of 10 shillings (50p). She refused to pay the fine imposed upon her when she was brought to court and so was imprisoned. Prisoners were divided into three divisions, according to their social standing. First Division prisoners were allowed many luxuries and could have food sent in from outside. In the lowest grade, Third Division, were ordinary, working-class men and women who were to expect no special privileges. Surprisingly, the First Division was still being used in prisons until 1948.

As soon as Wallace-Dunlop was sent to Holloway Prison, she asked to be treated as a political prisoner and placed in the First Division. When her requests to both the governor of the prison and also the Home Secretary were not immediately complied with, she announced that she would not eat until her crime was recognised as being political in nature and she had been put in the First Division. Today, we are quite familiar with political prisoners or imprisoned terrorists going on hunger strike in this way, but this was the first recorded use of a hunger strike for political purposes. That this can be a tremendously powerful weapon against the state has been amply demonstrated throughout the history of the twentieth century, from Mahatma Ghandi in colonial India to the IRA prisoner Bobby Sands in 1981.

Home Secretary Herbert Gladstone, keenly aware of the dangers of letting a suffragette prisoner kill herself in this way, ordered Wallace-Dunlop's release after she had refused all food for over 90 hours. The hunger strike was such a novelty that he made a spur of the moment decision, which the government later regretted. In no time at all, the tactic of the hunger strike had spread to many other WSPU members held in prison. Initially, others were also able to avail themselves of what was, in effect, a 'Get out of Gaol Free' card. Such a situation could not last for long and so the government, hoping to avoid women becoming martyrs, embarked upon the very strategy that was practically guaranteed to create them.

Inmates of lunatic asylums who refused to eat were sometimes forcibly fed, either by having their jaws prised open or by having rubber tubes pushed down their noses until they were in the patient's stomach. Milk, sometimes accompanied by raw eggs, was poured down the tube. The dangers of carrying out this procedure on struggling and uncooperative victims were very great. They ranged from cuts to the gums and broken teeth as the jaws were forced apart by steel gags, all the way to the risk of death when, as sometimes happened, the liquid was poured into the lungs and not the stomach. It is probable that some women later died from the after-effects of this treatment.

The powerful visual image of women being held down and forcibly fed has become one of the defining icons of the suffragette struggle. It was used to great effect on propaganda posters circulated by the WSPU, and the Liberal government of Asquith was, with some justification, accused of torturing women. This was a tremendous own goal for a government which had only used this method in order to avoid the creation of martyrs among the women they were holding.

Imprisoned suffragettes might have been denied the chance to die and so achieve martyrdom in that way, but they had now been handed a propaganda masterpiece where helpless women were having things forced into their bodies against their wishes. The comparison with rape was seldom explicitly stated, but hovered in the background of the debate on forced feeding. This visual image was exploited by the WSPU and had a very great impact. Posters featured distraught women being restrained while villainous-looking men wearing pince-nez inserted tubes into them.

Having shot themselves in the foot by setting out to force-feed women prisoners, with all the resultant sympathy this generated for them, the government then came up with another plan. The next scheme only made matters worse. The bind in which Asquith's government found itself was a tricky one. On the one hand, they did not wish for any of the suffragette prisoners to die. On the other, they were being portrayed as heartless brutes because of their use of force-feeding. The solution was to allow hunger strikers to be released on licence and then rearrested and taken back to prison to complete their sentences once they had recovered their health.

The Prisoners (Temporary Discharge for Ill Health) Act 1913 made provision for hunger strikers to be released and then later taken back to prison. It soon became known as the Cat and Mouse Act, due to the supposed similarity with a playful cat releasing and then catching a mouse with whom it is playing. Once more, it provided the WSPU with a brilliant image, that of a woman being held in the jaws of a gigantic cat. It was also a nightmare for the police to enforce, because as soon as suffragettes were temporarily released they would flee from sight. A network of supporters offered accommodation for fugitive prisoners who had been released under the Cat and Mouse Act. J.B. Priestley, in his book *The Edwardians*, compares the sheltering of such women with the 'underground railway' established during the American Civil War to care for runaway slaves.

There is no doubt that by using the weapon of the hunger strike, members of the WSPU were able to cultivate an impression of martyrdom, even if it fell short of the actual sacrifice of their lives. In time, the force-feeding in prisons resumed, because the law was being brought into disrepute. Suffragettes were being sentenced to prison and then freed within a matter of days. They would then flee and the police would have to waste time hunting them down in order to return them to prison for a short time, only for the process to begin anew.

Asquith's government had been hopelessly outmanoeuvred by the WSPU. Their attempts to avoid providing the suffragettes with their martyr had backfired in the most spectacular way and it was, in any case, all to be in vain. The suffragettes knew that they needed somebody to make the supreme sacrifice which would show to the world that they were serious in their devotion to this cause and that this devotion extended as far as giving their lives.

Some women had almost certainly already done this for the cause of women's suffrage. In 1910, Emmeline Pankhurst's sister, Mary Clark, was badly knocked about during a riot near the Houses of Parliament. She was arrested and imprisoned, but soon released. She died a short time later, probably of injuries received during the tussles with the police. There was however, nothing clear-cut and dramatic about the death of Mary Clark. What was needed was an obvious martyrdom, a woman giving her life for the suffragette cause.

Two months after the Cat and Mouse Act received Royal assent, a martyr duly appeared on behalf of those fighting for women's suffrage. That this disturbed and unhappy woman very nearly took somebody else's life as a result of her mad actions has been altogether forgotten. Today she lives on as the only suffragette that, apart from the Pankhursts, anybody can instantly remember.

Emily Wilding Davison secured her place in history as the woman who gave her life so that other women could get the vote. However, she is of interest not only for losing her life beneath the King's horse at Epsom, but also for the fact that she launched the arson and bombing campaigns which set the WSPU on the path of using terrorism to achieve their political ends. She was a violent and irrational woman, whose actions in the years leading up to her death at the age of 40 might encourage any objective observer to suspect that her most famous action was precipitated by factors other than merely strong political views.

Chapter Five

Emily Davison – Portrait of a Terrorist

❝ The government's refusal to grant the vote drove her to make her protest. Argument has not convinced Mr Asquith ... perhaps a woman's death will. ❞

(Christabel Pankhurst, *The Daily Sketch*, 1913)

On the evening of Saturday, 30 November 1912, a Baptist minister stood alone on a platform of Aberdeen's railway station. This inoffensive clergyman was about to become the victim of a senseless and brutal assault.

There was nothing remarkable or noteworthy about the Reverend Forbes Jackson, minister of the Crown Terrace Baptist Church in Aberdeen. He was just an ordinary, respectable man waiting quietly on the platform, minding his own business and bothering nobody. He could hardly have been more surprised when a middle-aged woman rushed up to him and began slashing him viciously across the face with a dog whip, shouting, 'I see through your disguise, Lloyd George. You cowardly hound, I'll punish you!'

This apparently mad woman was restrained by porters and handed over to the police. She gave her name as Mary Smith and explained that her reason for attacking the Reverend Jackson was because she believed that he was not a genuine clergyman at all, but was in reality none other than Chancellor of the Exchequer David Lloyd George, travelling under a convincing disguise! She did not tell the officers why she thought that one of the best known and most instantly recognisable men in the whole country should think it a good idea to put on a dog collar and try to pass himself off as a vicar.

By the time the case came to court, Mary Smith had, not unexpectedly, been revealed as a pseudonym or *nom de guerre*. The real name of the 40-year-old woman who had behaved so ferociously towards the innocent and law-abiding minister was Emily Davison and she was well-known to the police as one of the most militant of suffragettes.

Even now, a century after her violent death, Emily Davison is widely regarded as a secular saint in the struggle for women's rights. She is perhaps the only suffragette, other than the Pankhursts, whose name is still recognised a hundred years later by the average person. The scenes shot by the Pathé film crews at the 1913 Derby, showing Emily Davison falling beneath the hooves of the King's horse, are among the most iconic newsreel footage of the twentieth century. She is today revered in some quarters for her supposed martyrdom in the cause of women's rights.

In 2012, for example, a petition was organised calling for a minute's silence at the following year's Derby as a mark of respect for Emily Davison on the centenary of her actions at Derby Day in 1913. Among the founder members of this campaign was the General Secretary of the National Union of Teachers. Danny Boyle, who choreographed the opening ceremony of the 2012 Olympic Games, has said that the whole pageant was inspired by Emily Davison and her supposed martyrdom. Her death during the 1913 Derby Day was re-enacted during the opening ceremony, showing her being carried with her arms outstretched in a deliberate pastiche of Christian iconography; the audience were invited to compare her sacrifice with that of Christ.

Davison's name is still, for some at least, a byword for selfless devotion and readiness to sacrifice one's life for a just cause. This popular image is undeserved. She may well have thrown her own life away, but Emily Davison was far from being a gentle martyr. In fact, she was an extremely volatile and unpredictable woman, rootless and unemployed. She was responsible for injuring at least one person so severely that she almost faced a charge of causing grievous bodily harm, as well as being the first suffragette to use arson as a weapon and carrying out the first bomb attack in twentieth-century England. In many ways, Emily Davison epitomises the more aggressive type of suffragette who cheerfully engaged in acts of violence and destruction, giving no thought at all to those who might be injured or lose their lives in the process.

Emily Wilding Davison was born in South London on 11 October 1872. When she was three, her family moved to Hertfordshire and later back to London. A bright girl, she attended the Kensington High School where she did very well, both academically and in more athletic pursuits such as swimming, for which she won a gold medal. At the age of 19, she was awarded a bursary to study English at the Royal Holloway College. She later spent a term at Oxford University and then studied for an honours degree from the University of London.

After she had completed her studies, Emily Davison worked as a teacher and governess in various parts of the country. Before she was in her mid-thirties, there is no evidence that Davison took any interest in politics and it was not until the autumn of 1905, when she read about the imprisonment of Christabel Pankhurst and Annie Kenney, that she became intrigued by the new and militant form of suffragism which was being promoted. She was then 33 years old.

Over the next few years, Emily Davison was drawn into the activities of the WSPU. By 1908, she was acting as one of the chief stewards on the 'Women's Sunday' rally, which took place in Hyde Park that year. The following year, Davison was arrested for the first time and sent to prison for a month, after a protest at the Houses of Parliament.

In the summer of 1909, Emily Davison was back in prison for disrupting a meeting which was being addressed by Lloyd George. As soon as she was placed in her cell, she smashed 17 panes of glass. On being moved to another cell, she broke seven more. She had in fact brought a hammer into the prison but nobody had thought to search her. Later that year, Davison found herself in prison again, for disrupting a political meeting, and was subjected to force-feeding when she went on hunger strike. After this experience, she barricaded herself in her cell and the warders directed water from hoses through the window of the cell in an effort to subdue her.

During 1910, Emily Davison wrote articles for the suffragette newspaper *Votes for Women*, as well as sending innumerable letters to magazines and newspapers of all types, demanding that women be given the parliamentary vote. Twice that year, she received short prison sentences for breaking windows.

For most of 1911, the WSPU maintained a 'truce', abstaining from militant acts. This was in the expectation that a bill then passing through parliament could be amended to include a clause on women's suffrage. When the truce ended, Davison made the decision to ratchet up the violence by resorting to arson. This was the first time that this tactic had been used by the suffragettes and marks a new and dangerous departure from previous militant acts. It could be said that this was the moment at which the suffragettes moved from simple vandalism to the first stages of terrorism. The deliberate setting of fires has always been viewed as a grave crime, because of course flames are indiscriminate and uncontrollable. Once you begin a fire, there is no telling where or when it will stop. In later chapters we shall see how arson became a major weapon in the armoury of the WSPU, quite possibly leading to deaths. The first step though, taken by Emily Davison on Friday, 8 December 1911, was a small one.

On that particular morning, Davison went to the post office at 43 Fleet Street in London with a specially prepared package. This was cloth soaked in kerosene and contained in a paper envelope. A postbox was built into the front of the Fleet Street post office and after setting fire to her package, Emily Davison dropped the whole thing through the slot and into the post office. Fortunately, it went out almost immediately. Had it not done so, the consequences could have been serious, because the letters posted here all dropped down into a wooden box. Had the fire taken hold, the post office building, as well as those who worked in it, could have been in jeopardy.

When the letters from the Fleet Street post office were delivered to the Mount Pleasant sorting office later that day, the crude incendiary device was found, although nobody thought to report it. After seeing nothing about the attack in the newspapers over the weekend, Emily Davison marched up to Police Constable 185 on the following Monday and demanded to be arrested. He treated her as a crank and took no notice.

Later that week, on Thursday, 14 December, Davison set fire to two more pillar boxes in the City of London, one at Leadenhall Street and the other near the Mansion House. Then she went to Whitehall and tried to set fire to the post office in Parliament Street by putting a lighted match to some kerosene-soaked rags, which she hoped to push into the postbox set into the front of the building. She was caught in the act by a policeman and taken to nearby Scotland Yard, where she freely confessed what she had done. Later that day, Emily Davison was taken to Cannon Row police station and charged with arson.

In January 1912, Davison was tried at the Old Bailey and sent to prison for six months for arson, a lenient sentence given the nature of the crime. It was while in prison for this offence that Emily Davison's mind turned, according to her own account, to self-destruction. It is impossible to know what prompted these thoughts. The motive may have been purely political or maybe she was a disturbed woman with little to live for, someone who thought that although her life was pointless, her death could serve some purpose. The events of this time in prison have a good deal of bearing on what subsequently befell this unhappy woman.

There were a fair number of suffragettes in London's Holloway Prison at the time that Emily Davison was serving her sentence there for arson. As before, she went on hunger strike, along with other prisoners. On 22 June, the suffragette prisoners decided to barricade themselves in their cells as a protest against the continued force-feeding to which they were being subjected. The prison authorities managed to get through the cell doors and resume the force-feeding, after which Davison smashed the remaining panes of glass in her cell. She decided that if she gave her life, 'One big tragedy may save many others' (her own words). The cell in which Davison was confined was on the top floor of the prison wing, with the door leading out on to a narrow walkway which overlooked a considerable drop.

When her cell door was opened later that afternoon, Emily Davison rushed out of the cell and threw herself over the railings. Her intention was to fall to her death in the central hall of the prison. In her excitement, she had apparently forgotten that wire netting was stretched over the hall at the level of the first floor for the very purpose of frustrating suicides of this sort. The warders brought her back up the stairs, whereupon she dived over the railings once more, trying to fall away from the edge of the wire netting, so that she could land on an iron staircase. Once more, she ended up on the wire netting, her frantic bid for suicide rapidly descending into farce. At last she succeeded in injuring herself though, as before the warders were able to retrieve her once more from the wire netting, she jumped head first onto the iron staircase, a drop of 10 feet or so. Davison landed on her head, knocking herself out.

There cannot be the slightest doubt that Emily Davison, a year before her death at the Derby, was genuinely trying to end her life. She wrote later of this episode in Holloway, 'If I had been successful, I should undoubtedly have been killed'. It is hard to imagine a clearer statement of an intended suicide than this.

The final dive, head first onto the iron staircase, resulted in concussion and two cracked vertebrae in Davison's spine. She was plagued by pains from these injuries for the rest of her life.

After her release, following her suicide attempt, Emily Davison resumed her activities on behalf of the suffragettes. Which brings us to the extraordinary attack on the Reverend Jackson at Aberdeen Railway Station. Lloyd George was giving a speech in Aberdeen in November 1912, but the Chancellor of the Exchequer would hardly travel to and from London alone. As for the idea that he would do so in fancy dress, pretending to be a vicar, it is safe to assume that no well-balanced person would entertain this notion for a moment. But was Emily Davison well-balanced at that time? The evidence tends to suggest otherwise.

There is a common misconception that Emily Davison was a young woman when she died, shortly after that fateful Derby. Accounts of her life often aim deliberately to give this impression, perhaps because a girl sacrificing her life is more likely to tug at the heart-strings than the death of an older woman. The official website of the *BBC History* magazine, for instance, has a piece on the suffragettes which states: 'As the government struggled to prevent scores dying in prison, one young woman successfully provided the cause with its first martyr. In

June 1913, Emily Davison was killed by the King's horse at the Epsom Derby'. Davison was a few months short of her forty-first birthday when she died, hardly a 'young woman' by the standards of the time.

What sort of life did Davison lead in the weeks and months leading up to her death? Stripped of a century's hagiography, Emily Davison's life was not an enviable one. She had no family of her own, was unemployed and her health was poor. She had been in and out of prison for the last couple of years, which did not make getting a job any easier; indeed, it rendered her all but unemployable as a governess or teacher. Without the struggle for female emancipation, she would have been eking out a wretched, hand-to-mouth existence, with no prospect of any improvement in her life as she grew older. She was wholly dependent upon the charity of friends, having no resources at all of her own.

A letter written to an old school friend gives some insight into her life in the early part of 1913. She wrote:

> *I am at present with my mother, who is glad to have me ... The last four days' hunger strike in Aberdeen have, of course, found out my weakness, and I have had some rheumatism in my neck and back, where I fell on that iron staircase. If it is wet or I am tired, both parts ache ... At present I have no settled work here or in town ... I wish I could hear of some work though.*

Davison was constantly applying for jobs right up to her death, without success. Her family were evidently a little bitter about the fact that, although she had devoted her life to the suffragette cause, the WSPU would not give her a salaried position. Sending her a postal order, one family member said in the letter which accompanied this gift of money, 'I do think the militants might remember your services and give you something'.

In the next chapter, we shall look in detail at the bombing of Lloyd George's house at Walton-on-the-Hill. According to Sylvia Pankhurst, writing almost 20 years after the event, the bombing of Lloyd George's house was carried out by Emily Davison and others. Sylvia Pankhurst was in the best possible position to know about it and had no conceivable reason to lie. This shows Davison to have been very careless not only of her own life, but also those of other people. The bomb exploded only 20 minutes or so before a group of workmen arrived at the house. Those who planted that bomb really did not care whether or not they harmed others in the process.

Sylvia Pankhurst was not the only associate of Emily Davison to know about her forays into terrorism. More evidence is to be found in the words of one of her close friends, Edith Mansell-Moullin, who, together with her husband, was closely involved with the campaign for women's suffrage and who wrote an account of Emily Davison's life. Before doing so, she asked, in a letter to a mutual friend, whether she should, 'leave out the bombs?' The fact that this close friend and Sylvia Pankhurst both thought that Davison had been handling bombs puts the matter beyond reasonable doubt. Both thought very highly of Davison and neither had any reason for inventing such a thing.

And so we come to that most famous incident in Emily Davison's life, the only event in her life of which most people have even heard. On 4 June 1913, she bought a return ticket to Epsom. Earlier that day, she had visited the WSPU offices to pick up two suffragette flags in green, white and purple. When asked why she needed them, she was evasive. She told one woman that if she read the evening paper that day, then she might see something about the business.

Much has been made about the significance of Davison's choosing to buy a return ticket to Epsom as though this sheds some light upon her state of mind. In fact, for excursions to Derby Day, it was no cheaper to buy a single ticket than it was to purchase a return. Besides, even if Emily Davison had been intending only a protest which would not entail her own death, she would surely have realised that arrest was inevitable. Whatever she planned, it must have been pretty clear when she bought that return ticket that she would not in fact be using the return half. Either she would be in a police cell, hospital or mortuary.

In later years, stories emerged that Davison, perhaps in the company of friends, had practised grabbing horses and attaching things to their bridles. Shortly before the Derby, she had visited the village of Longhorsely, not far from her mother's home in Northumberland. While there, she had supposedly been seen at Longhorsely racecourse, trying to grab the bridles of moving horses. It is worth noting that this story did not come to light until years after Davison's death. The idea that it would be possible to attach a flag to the bridle of a horse travelling at 30 or 40 miles an hour is so preposterous that it may probably be discounted. If that was really the object of the exercise when Emily Davison went to the 1913 Derby, then it suggests that her mental state was even more fragile than anybody could have guessed.

Once she arrived at Epsom, Davison made her way to the racecourse and positioned herself at Tattenham Corner, which was where the Pathé newsreel cameras were filming the race. Whether this was deliberate or mere coincidence, it means that we have a filmed record of what happened when the horses thundered round the bend. Most of the riders had passed, leaving four or five trailing behind. One of these was the King's horse, Anmar, ridden by Herbert Jones. The figure of a woman ducks under the barrier and runs out onto the racetrack. One horse swerves slightly and avoids her. Then the woman raises both arms above her head and appears to be standing in front of, or clutching at Anmar. When a horse weighing half a ton and travelling at 35 miles an hour hits a human body under such circumstances, the result will surprise nobody. The woman is knocked under the flying hooves and as the animal's legs become tangled up, it trips and performs a somersault, throwing the rider and landing on top of him.

In recent years, there has been much debate as to Emily Davison's intentions that day. Was she trying to get herself killed or was her aim only to disrupt the race? Could she have been trying to pin one of the suffragette flags to the horse's reins, or possibly slip a scarf over its head, so that the King's horse carried the green, white and purple colours past the finishing line? A scarf in the suffragette colours was found near her. Might she have hoped to loop this round the horse's neck as it thundered past?

In 2013, the centenary of her death, a television documentary subjected the film of that fateful Derby to modern analysis. It was claimed that this showed clearly that Davison was trying to grab at or pin something on the horse's reins and not throw herself deliberately beneath the horse at all.

The debates about Emily Davison's precise motives on Derby Day 1913 miss the point. Her intentions are, in a sense, irrelevant; it is her actions which show what sort of person she was and these indicate that she did not care who she harmed that day. She chose to run in front of and interfere with a galloping horse carrying a rider, thereby not only risking her own life, but also that of whoever was riding the horse. Her own injuries were certainly caused by her actions, but there was another victim of her behaviour, one who is almost never mentioned in accounts of the incident.

It was little short of a miracle that Herbert Jones, the jockey of the horse in front of which Davison ran, was also not killed that day. His horse turned a complete somersault and landed on top of him. In the

MILITANCY TO GO ON.

IRISH CATHEDRAL DAMAGED BY DYNAMITE.

Newspaper headline on the first terrorist bombing in Ulster of the twentieth century; carried out
•t by the IRA but by the suffragettes.

2. Memorial plaque to Alice Wheeldon, the
suffragette convicted at the Old Bailey of
conspiring to murder the Prime Minister.

DERBY CIVIC SOCIETY

ALICE WHEELDON

1866 - 1919

Anti-war activist,
socialist and suffragist

lived here behind
her shop

DERBY CITY COUNCIL

3. Glorifying terrorism: the inscription at the
base of Emmeline Pankhurst's statue,
commemorating the militant campaign.

These Walls and Piers have
been erected in Memory of
Dame Christabel Pankhurst
who jointly with her Mother
Mrs Emmeline Pankhurst
inspired and led the
Militant Suffrage Campaign

4. The statue of Emmeline Pankhurst, leader of the suffragettes, who was convicted at the Old Bailey of inciting a terrorist bomb attack against the house of the Chancellor of the Exchequer.

5. Emily Davison, pictured a few weeks befor she inflicted GBH on a complete stranger.

6. Death of a terrorist: Emily Davison was mortally injured at the 1913 Derby.

THE DERBY TRAGEDY : AT TATTEN
A SUFFRAGETTE'S MAD RUSH AND ITS C

The shooting gallery in London's
Tottenham Court Road, where would-be
suffragette assassins honed their skills with
semi-automatic pistols.

8. Lincoln's Inn House, the London headquarters of
the Women's Social and Political Union, where the
bombings and arson attacks were coordinated.

'Votes for Women' badge: some suggested that 'Votes for ladies' might have been a more
appropriate slogan for the socially exclusive suffragettes.

10. The true cost of suffragette militancy: a number of women lost their jobs as a result of the attack on this teahouse at Kew Gardens.

11. Saunderton Railway Station was destroyed by the suffragettes as part of their campaign of terror against the transport infrastructure in 1913.

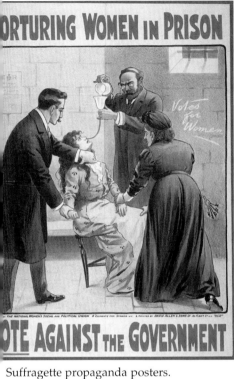

Suffragette propaganda posters.

13. A typical suffragette terrorist: Mabel Capper (pictured centre) took part in bombings and arson.

14. Christabel Pankhurst: architect of the bombing campaign.

Damage to a house near Holloway Prison, after the suffragettes set off two explosions near the son.

Fascist leader Oswald Mosley: his party seemed the natural home for many former suffragettes.

THE SUSPECTED SEX.

Stationmaster-cum-porter of wayside "Halt." "'ERE, BILL, JUST KEEP AN EYE ON THE OLE GAL ON THE PLATFORM WHILST I GETS MY DINNER."
Bill. "WHOFFOR? SHE CAN'T COME TO NO 'ARM."
Stationmaster. "I'M NOT THINKIN' OF 'ER 'EALTH, I'M THINKIN' ABOUT MY STATION. SHE MIGHT WANT TO BURN IT DOWN."

17. Behind the propaganda: how the suffragettes were often viewed by ordinary people.

MILITANTS BLOW UP CORONATION CHAIR

Bomb in Westminster Abbey Wrecks Historic Relic and Damages Altar Screen.

NEW PLAN TO END OUTRAGES

Government to Prosecute Civilly and Criminally Subscribers to Suffragette War Chest.

Special Cable to THE NEW YORK TIMES.

18. June 1914: the climax of the suffragette bombings.

event he suffered only concussion and a dislocated shoulder. The legal position when somebody behaves in such a dangerous fashion though is quite clear. Emily Davison was legally and morally responsible for the injuries to the jockey. She had evidently not cared in the least if somebody else was hurt as a consequence of what she did. While she was lying unconscious in hospital, the Director of Public Prosecutions announced that 'if Miss Davison recovers, it will be possible to charge her with doing an act calculated to cause grievous bodily harm'.

One more detail is usually left out of the reckoning when Emily Davison's story is recounted today: that she was without doubt guilty of inflicting GBH upon Jones, a man with whom she could have no possible quarrel. Combining this with the unprovoked attack on the Reverend Jackson, the attempted arson at two post offices and the bombing of Lloyd George's house we have a more rounded portrait of the suffragettes' most famous heroine.

Herbert Jones said in later years that he was 'haunted by that poor woman's face' and he was greatly affected psychologically by Davison's death beneath the hooves of his horse. He himself committed suicide many years later and there is at least a suspicion that his inadvertent role in Emily Davison's death was connected with his own suicide.

Reading the contemporary newspaper accounts of this race is a disconcerting experience today. In retrospect, the only possible point of interest that day can surely have been Emily Davison's behaviour? Even *The Times* was more concerned with the fact that the favourite, Craganour, although the first horse past the post, was subsequently disqualified by a stewards' enquiry and the race given to Aboyeur. It was the first time in many years that such a thing had happened at a Derby and for most newspaper readers this was of far more consequence than another suffragette protest.

The suffragettes had finally found the martyr they needed and Emily Davison's funeral was turned into a grand exercise in propaganda. The inquest into her death, held in Guildford on 10 June, brought in a verdict of accidental death from a fractured skull, caused by 'being accidentally knocked down by a horse through wilfully rushing onto the race course at Epsom Downs Surrey on the 4th June 1913, during the progress of a race'.

For the WSPU it was infinitely more advantageous to depict her as a suicide and martyr to the cause of women's suffrage, than to have her death treated as merely an accident. Writing in the popular newspaper, the *Daily Sketch*, Christabel Pankhurst said that, 'The government's refusal to grant the vote drove her to make her protest. Argument has not convinced Mr Asquith of the seriousness of the position, but perhaps a woman's death will'.

It was plain that the WSPU intended to milk this death for all that it was worth. Not unnaturally, Emily Davison's mother in Northumberland wanted her daughter to be buried near to her, but it was still possible for the WSPU to make capital from the death by an ostentatious funeral procession in the capital. It would be interesting to know what Mrs Davison made of this attempt to wring every advantage from her daughter's death. She seemed herself to regard the suffragette movement with a certain amount of disfavour, at least in their dealings with her daughter. She could not have expected her daughter to die, because she wrote a letter to her at the hospital in Epsom, saying, 'I cannot believe that you could have done such a dreadful act, even for the cause which I know you have given up your heart and soul to. It has done so little in return for you'.

It would also be interesting to know why Mrs Davison thought that the cause had done, 'so little', for her daughter. There were hints after her death that the leadership of the WSPU regarded the over-zealous Emily Davison with a certain reserve and did not feel that she was really one of them. She was never given a paid role in the organisation, which meant that she was constantly struggling for money.

Her body was brought from Epsom to Victoria Station and transported across London to Kings Cross, where it travelled north to Davison's mother's home. A spectacular parade was laid on through central London, with mourners dressed in the suffragettes' colours marching along behind the hearse. What the dead woman's mother would have made of this exploitation of her daughter's death can only be imagined. Between Emily Davison's action at the Derby and her funeral in Northumberland on 15 June, there were a number of suffragette attacks, including one which caused over £7,000 worth of damage at another racecourse.

On the night of 8 June, a patrolling police constable noticed flames coming from some wooden buildings at Hurst Park. An off-duty fireman gave evidence that he had seen two women heading towards Hurst Park at about 10.45 pm. They were each carrying a bag, but when seen later had nothing in their hands. Copies of *The Suffragette* were found near the burned-out stand at the race track.

When the police learned that the WSPU had it in mind to hold a spectacular demonstration to coincide with the transfer of Emily Davison's body from Victoria Station, where it was due to arrive from Epsom, to King's Cross (where it would be returned to her mother's home town of Morpeth) there was some uneasiness. They suspected, quite correctly as it turned out, that the suffragettes were planning to exploit the passage of the body through central London for political ends. Writing on behalf of the Commissioner of Police for the Metropolis, Chief Clerk, W.H. Kendall sent a letter to Mary Allen, who was organising the procession for the WSPU. In it, he wrote:

> *Madam, – Having regard to the traffic conditions in the streets through which the funeral procession has to pass, I am directed to warn you that as all reasonable facilities must be given to the ordinary traffic, the progress of the proposed funeral cortege may be greatly hindered, and if the crowd of sightseers is more than usually large, it may prove impractical for the hearse to reach the church in time for the service there. In order to convey the remains from one railway station to another in a seemly and reverent manner, the hearse should be accompanied by a limited number of mourners only and taken through streets where traffic conditions will not interfere with its progress. The police will be prepared to indicate a suitable route.*

This is a curious letter. It sounds very much as though the police feared that the suffragettes would be turning Emily Davison's funeral into a three ring circus; references to a 'crowd of sightseers' and the need for a 'seemly and reverential manner' certainly appear to hint at such an attitude.

That the police proved themselves prescient on this point may be seen from the actual arrangements made for what was destined to be the last great public display by the WSPU. The advice that the hearse should be 'taken through streets where traffic conditions will not interfere with its progress' was hardly adhered to, as the procession behind the hearse passed through some of the busiest streets in the capital, including Piccadilly Circus, Shaftesbury Avenue and Euston Road. Nor were 'a limited number of mourners' involved. The WSPU worked frantically to ensure that as many of their members as were able came to London for the day. Traffic came to a standstill on Saturday, 14 June, as apart from the many suffragettes marching behind the hearse, thousands of people thronged the streets to watch the show.

The cynicism of the WSPU in using Emily Davison's death in this way as a propaganda coup can be more readily appreciated when we learn that her mother, who was intending to bury her daughter in Northumberland on the following day, very nearly had to cancel the funeral arrangements. The suffragettes held a service of their own at St George's Church in Bloomsbury and what with the high numbers of mourners that they had laid on and the crowds they had courted, combined with a route which passed deliberately through the most congested streets of the capital; everything took far longer than had been planned for. The train that was scheduled to carry Davison's remains to Northumberland was due to leave King's Cross at 5.30 pm. The grand spectacle laid on by the WSPU took so long that the coffin arrived at King's Cross precisely one minute before the train left. The coffin was hurriedly loaded on board the train in a manner which was anything but 'seemly and reverential'. Two minutes more and Mrs Davison would not have been able to bury her child on the day of her choice.

This then was the life and death of the first suffragette arsonist and bomber. A seemingly disturbed and aggressive woman who at 40 had no permanent home of her own and was constantly hard up and unable to get a job. Who, in her right mind, could honestly believe that the Chancellor of the Exchequer would travel about the country dressed as a clergyman? Who, except somebody quite heedless of the lives of others would try to block the path of a galloping horse? When looked at without prejudice, it is hard to disagree with the sentiments expressed by Queen Mary when writing to the unfortunate Herbert Jones. She commiserated with him on his, 'sad accident caused through the abominable conduct of a brutal, lunatic woman'.

Although the WSPU had worked long and hard to find themselves a suitable martyr who could be manipulated as part of a public relations exercise to blacken the name of Asquith and his government, reactions were not all that could have been desired. It is true that the actions of Emily Davison garnered a huge amount of publicity for the suffragette cause and captured the front pages of all the newspapers. Whether by accident or design, Emily Davison chose the perfect spot to carry out her mad protest. Not only were there many newspaper photographers on hand, the newsreel cameras were also running and film of the incident appeared in cinemas across the country. Emily Davison, and of course the cause for which she died, became tremendously famous overnight. Her funeral procession through central London was also a media event, lapped up by the papers and newsreels.

Getting publicity is one thing, ensuring that those viewing that publicity take away with them the right message is something else again. Emily Davison's death changed the way that people regarded the suffragettes in two very different ways. On the one hand, it was undeniable that here was a cause for which people had now shown that they were prepared to sacrifice their lives. This is a sobering reflection, whatever you might personally feel about a cause for which a life has been given. The other change in perspective was not so desirable for the WSPU. The question began to be asked, if this is how a highly intelligent, middle-aged university graduate behaves, what does this tell us about the fitness of women to have the vote? If even the most educated, older women are liable to carry on like this, whatever must the mental state of the uneducated, younger ones be like? Were all the suffragettes as unbalanced as this?

There was a bizarre sequel to Emily Davison's act at the 1913 Derby, which did nothing to dispel the idea that such behaviour verged on lunacy. Most people in Britain today are vaguely aware of Emily Davison's name and the protest for which she is remembered, but few now recall the name of Harry Hewitt. This is surprising, because two weeks after Emily Davison's protest, Harry Hewitt did precisely the same thing, under similar circumstances and perhaps for the same reason.

The next major horse racing event after the 1913 Derby was the Ascot Gold Cup, held on 19 June. It was a beautiful summer's day and most people had forgotten all about the unfortunate incident at the Derby. Herbert Jones, the jockey who had been injured by Emily Davison, had recovered and was attending the Gold Cup as a spectator. As the horses came into the final curve before they thundered past the stands, Tracery, ridden by Albert 'Snowy' Whalley, was in the lead. A smartly dressed man, wearing a grey suit, ducked under the fence surrounding the track and walked calmly out in front of the horses. He looked so respectable, that many in the watching crowd formed the impression that he was an official, connected in some way with the race. Then, he produced a suffragette flag in one hand and a revolver in the other and ran straight into the path of the leading horse.

What followed was virtually a carbon copy of the Derby. Tracery crashed into the man, knocking him down and then the horse itself went down, throwing Albert Whalley in the process. The following horses managed to avoid the tangled group, although one of them clipped the man who had disrupted the race with its hoof.

The jockey suffered from concussion, but Harry Hewitt, the man who had made the protest, needed surgery, a piece of bone having been driven into his brain by the kick he received from one of the horses. He was later removed to an asylum, from which he escaped and fled to Canada. Pity poor Herbert Jones, who had come to spend a day at the races largely in order to forget about his role in Emily Davison's death. The copycat incident at Ascot showed how easily one irrational person can encourage others who are slightly unbalanced to emulate them.

A century has passed since the death of Emily Davison, the first of the WSPU's arsonists and bombers. We are now in a position to make a fairly balanced and objective judgement about the woman and her actions at the 1913 Derby after the passage of so much time, but the verdict is not a favourable one to her. We know that Emily Davison inflicted grievous bodily harm upon Herbert Jones, the King's jockey. There is also no doubt that she was willing to slash a complete stranger across the face with a whip, because he bore a passing resemblance to a well-known politician. This same woman did not hesitate to detonate 5 lbs of explosives in such a way that there was an excellent chance of killing somebody. In the course of this action, she deprived an ordinary, working man of his livelihood. Not only that, she also tried to set fire to two post offices.

It is almost beyond belief that a century later, such a woman as this could be put forward as somebody deserving of our admiration and respect. The very name, 'Emily Davison', is spoken reverently, as though it is taken as read that she was a remarkable, and indeed wonderful, human being. In one way at least, Emily Davison was indeed remarkable. She was a pioneer of terrorism, being the first suffragette in England to resort to arson and bombing to further the aims of the WSPU. Where Davison led, others followed. The bombing of Lloyd George's house was the opening shot in a campaign of violence which swept the country during the course of 1913 and 1914.

Chapter Six

Bombing and Arson

*⟨ If any woman refrains from militant protest
against the injury done by the Government and
the House of Commons against women ... she
will share responsibility for the crime. ⟩*

(Emmeline Pankhurst, 10 January, 1913)

There had, from 1911 onwards, been sporadic and isolated attempts at arson and even, as at the Theatre Royal in Dublin, the occasional use of explosives by members of the WSPU. However, the campaign of bombing and arson began in earnest on 19 February 1913.

Chancellor of the Exchequer David Lloyd George was probably, for the suffragettes, the most hated man in the government besides Herbert Asquith. Why this should have been the case is something of a mystery. He was a dedicated supporter of the principle of women's suffrage, although not enthusiastic about the Pankhursts' idea of 'equal suffrage'.

In early 1913 Lloyd George was having a house built for himself near the golf course at Walton-on-the-Hill in Surrey. The men working on the house arrived each morning at 6.30 am and left at 5.30 pm On the evening of 18 February, the workmen left as usual in the evening and secured the property behind them. There was, however, one small and unfinished window on the ground floor which could not be fully closed. It was later guessed that a boy, or slim woman, might have been able to squeeze through this window and then possibly open another window to let in accomplices.

Cars were something of a rarity at that time and a number of witnesses were woken by the sound of a motor vehicle driving to Walton in the early hours of the morning of 19 February. The car was also heard by a police officer, who noted that it arrived in Walton at about 2.50 am. The sound of a car was sufficiently uncommon to draw attention, particularly at night. He also heard a vehicle, possibly the same one, driving back towards London two hours later. It was unusual to hear a car driving about at that time, but nothing more was thought of it.

At 6.10 am, the windows of the Blue Ball pub in Walton were rattled by a loud explosion. Twenty minutes later, James Grey, foreman of the builders, arrived at the house that he and his men had almost completed and found a scene of devastation. The ceilings had been brought down by an explosion, windows blown out and the force of the blast had even cracked open an external brick wall. Five rooms were wrecked. The police were called and discovered that two bombs had been planted in the house. The method used to trigger the explosions was primitive in the extreme. A paraffin-soaked rag led from the bomb to a saucer of wood shavings, which had also been sprinkled with paraffin. A candle was then placed in this saucer and lit. When it burned down far enough, it set fire to the wood shavings and then ignited the rag which acted as a fuse.

Two bombs had actually been planted in the house, but the explosion of the first had blown out the candle which was meant to trigger the second. This meant that the Home Office explosives expert was able to examine in detail the construction of the bombs. The unexploded bomb consisted of 5 lbs of gunpowder, surrounded with nails to make it more destructive. Anybody who had been in the house at the time of the explosion would have stood a good chance of being killed.

Scotland Yard sent officers from the Special Branch to investigate this latest outrage, which represented a serious escalation in political violence. There were few clues, other than the discovery of two hairpins and a galosh. The leaving of hairpins at the scene of such attacks was to become something of a hallmark of the suffragette bombers and arsonists.

The explosion at Lloyd George's house had been preceded less than a week before by the burning down of the refreshment shed at Regents Park Cricket Ground in London. After this attack, incidents of arson and sabotage increased dramatically across the whole country. On 12 February, the Tea House at Kew Gardens was burned to the ground. Two days later, Ashford Golf Course was damaged and on 24 February, telegraph poles in Newcastle were cut down. That same day, signal wires were cut on various railway lines. On the following day, telephone wires were cut in Belfast and a bookstall was burned to the ground in Staffordshire. The usual round of window-smashing, letter-burning and other acts of vandalism were continuing throughout the country.

March brought new and even more serious arson attacks. On 9 March, two railway stations, Saunderton and Croxley Green, were destroyed by fire and on 12 March, a fire was started in a lavatory at the British Museum. On 21 March, the house of Lady White at Englefield Green was burned down and on the same day the golf pavilion at Weston-Super-Mare was also destroyed by fire. Two days later, telephone wires were cut and many yards of them removed near Hull. On 24 March, extensive damage was caused to Sandwich golf links.

Some of the targets are predictable enough for a guerrilla campaign – the transport system and communications infrastructure, for instance. But where do cricket grounds and golf courses fit into the pattern? In fact, they are part of the same overall scheme as Emily Davison's actions at the Derby. To see what was going on, it is necessary to look at what Emmeline Pankhurst had to say at her trial in early April that year and also to consider the writings of her daughter Christabel from exile in Paris.

The police had been unable to track down and arrest those who had actually planted the bomb at Lloyd George's house. Sylvia Pankhurst, writing long after the event, claimed that Emily Davison was one of the bombers, although the police had other suspects in mind. Nevertheless, there was no doubt, at least as far as the government was concerned, where ultimate responsibility for this act of terrorism lay and that was with the leadership of the WSPU.

Emmeline Pankhurst in particular, had since the beginning of 1913, been sailing exceedingly close to the wind. On 10 January that year, she wrote to members of the WSPU. Heading the letter, 'Private and Confidential', this was, to all intents and purposes, a call to arms. After discussing the situation in parliament, Mrs Pankhurst went on to say:

There are degrees of militancy. Some women are able to go further than others in militant action and each woman is the judge of her own duty so far as that is concerned. To be militant in some way or other is, however, a moral obligation. It is a duty which every woman owes to her conscience and self-respect, to other women who are less fortunate than she is herself, and to all those who are to come after her.

If any woman refrains from militant protest against the injury done by the Government and the House of Commons against women and to the race, she will share responsibility for the crime. Submission under such circumstances will be itself a crime. We must, as I have said, prepare to meet the crisis before it arises. Will you therefore tell me (by letter if it is not possible to do so by word of mouth), that you are ready to take your share in manifesting in a practical manner your indignation at the betrayal of our cause.

Yours sincerely,

E Pankhurst.

Even before this, Mrs Pankhurst had already openly encouraged illegal actions such as smashing windows. At a public meeting at the Albert Hall in October 1912, she had said, 'Those of you who can break windows, break them. Those of you who can still further attack the sacred idol of property ... do so'.

The general public had on the whole been indifferent to the suffragette campaign. As long as it was limited to heckling cabinet ministers and breaking windows in Downing Street, most people were happy to ignore them. Once the smashing of whole streets of shop windows began and buildings began to be burned down, the mood changed. When the WSPU held their rally for 'Women's Sunday' in 1908, thousands of people came to Hyde Park to see what all the fuss was about. They may not have become active supporters, but they came with open minds and some probably left with a more favourable attitude towards female emancipation than when they arrived. This changed dramatically once the arson and bombing began.

A month after the bombing of Lloyd George's house, the WSPU held a rally in Hyde Park. The meeting, on 17 March, quickly degenerated into a riot. The suffragettes had complained often enough in the past about the heavy-handed tactics of the police at their meetings; on this occasion, they were grateful that so many police were in attendance. The mood of the crowd was decidedly ugly and none of the speakers could be heard above the catcalls and angry shouts. The heckling and abuse had nothing to do with the WSPU's demand for the parliamentary vote. Instead, the cries were 'Incendiary!' and 'Shopbreakers!' Clods of earth were dug up and thrown and women grabbed and manhandled. The fury of the mob was concerned solely with the acts of militancy and had no reference at all to political questions. By adopting a policy of violence against privately owned property, the leadership of the WSPU had succeeded in transforming public indifference into outright hostility and ill will. A suffragette open air meeting at Wimbledon also descended into chaos a day or two later and for the same reason: anger over widespread vandalism and arson.

After the bombing at Walton-on-the-Hill, Emmeline Pankhurst at once announced that she was responsible for the explosion. She repeated this assertion in an article published in *The Suffragette*, the newspaper of the WSPU and on 24 February, she was arrested and charged with 'Feloniously procuring and inciting a person or persons unknown to commit felony, unlawfully soliciting and inciting persons unknown to commit felony and certain misdemeanours'.

The trial opened at the Old Bailey on 1 April, 1913. Transcripts of various speeches that Emmeline Pankhurst had made were produced in evidence, the prosecution suggesting that these were 'soliciting and inciting' others to commit felonies. The letter in January in which Mrs Pankhurst had urged all women to take part in militancy was also read out.

Emmeline Pankhurst did not defend herself in the conventional way, but instead made a long and rambling speech to the judge and jury. Very little of this speech was relevant to the charge against her and some of it was very strange indeed. Among other things, Mrs Pankhurst reminded the court that she had been married to a barrister and that her dead husband had told her some shocking tales about the behaviour of men in high places. She began to tell the story of a judge who had been found dead in a brothel, but at this point, was warned that she must not name anybody and that it would be better to restrict her comments to the charge against her.

It is unlikely that this anecdote about the immoral judge did anything to endear the defendant to the judge trying her own case, but Mrs Pankhurst had more to say on the depravity of men. She continued:

Only this morning I have had information brought to me which could be supported by sworn affidavits, that there is in this country, in this very city of London of ours, a regulated traffic, not only in women of full age, but in little children, that they are being purchased, that they are being entrapped, and that they are being trained to minister to the vicious pleasures of persons who ought to know better in their positions of life.

The judge was determined to offer Emmeline Pankhurst as much leeway as he possibly could, but like most of those present in court that day, he must have begun seriously to wonder about the mental state of somebody being tried for an offence of this nature and seemingly unable to understand what was going on. After threatening to go on hunger strike if she was convicted, Mrs Pankhurst made one last, bizarre statement. She said of the suffragettes that, 'They know that the very fount of life is being poisoned, they know that homes are being destroyed, that because of bad education, because of the unequal standard of morals, even the mothers and children are destroyed by one of the vilest and most horrible diseases that ravage humanity'. It did not take the jury long to find Emmeline Pankhurst guilty, although with a strong recommendation to mercy. She was sent to prison for three years.

Most people, finding themselves standing in the dock at the Old Bailey and charged with inciting acts of terrorism, might perhaps not behave quite as Mrs Pankhurst did on that April day a little over a century ago. Readers will probably wonder what on earth was going through her mind as she gave that speech to the court. 'Vicious pleasures', 'horrible diseases', 'fount of life is being poisoned', dead judges in brothels, what was it all about? It certainly had no connection with the bomb explosion at the house of the Chancellor of the

Exchequer, which of course had led to her appearance at the Old Bailey. Nor did 'horrible diseases' and 'vicious pleasures' appear to have anything to do with the charge that Mrs Pankhurst faced of inciting persons unknown to commit a felony.

To understand Emmeline Pankhurst's behaviour in court, we must see what Christabel Pankhurst had been doing in Paris while she was in exile. Only then will we be able to understand both what caused Emmeline Pankhurst to talk so oddly at her trial and also to find out how this is connected with the burning down of cricket pavilions, the blowing up of football grounds, the destruction of golf courses and, of course, Emily Davison's strange actions at that year's Derby.

From the middle of 1912 onwards, the leaders of the WSPU became convinced that the refusal to grant women the parliamentary vote was a crime against the race. We saw Emmeline Pankhurst hint at this in her letter to the members of the WSPU, when she talked of the injury done by the government, 'against women and to the race'. Her daughter Christabel explained this passing reference in detail in articles published in *The Suffragette* throughout 1913. Her pieces on this subject were collected together and published later that year, as a book called *The Great Scourge and How to End It*.

Briefly, the thesis advanced by the Pankhursts, mother and daughter, was as follows: The great majority of men in Britain, Christabel claimed the figure to be between 75 and 80 per cent, were infected with sexually transmitted diseases such as gonorrhoea. They frequently picked up these diseases through visiting prostitutes, which the Pankhursts referred to coyly as the 'Social Evil'. One consequence of this was that they passed on gonorrhoea to their wives, causing them to become sterile or to give birth to deformed babies. This was described as 'race suicide'. Another wicked side-effect of men's insatiable sexual appetites was that a constant supply of prostitutes had to be created by means of the 'white slavery' racket, whereby young girls were abducted and forced into prostitution.

From late 1912, these bizarre ideas became official doctrine of the WSPU. The only way to save the race and also protect women from the infections with which men were riddled was to allow women an active role in politics. They would soon put a stop to these disgusting practices!

It seems incredible now that sort of thing could have been taken seriously by anybody, even a century ago. Such seemingly outlandish ideas did no good for the suffragette cause and not only with those who opposed them. As the WSPU increasingly portrayed the struggle for women's suffrage as a moral crusade to save the race from extinction and little girls from the white slavers, so their membership went into free fall. It was not only men who recognised this rhetoric to be nonsense, even many women who had stuck with the WSPU for years began to become disillusioned with it.

This brings us to the question of the burning of cricket pavilions and the disruption of the Derby by Emily Davison. Those who might be wondering what sort of political act an attack on the golf course at Weston-Super-Mare might be, or about the bomb that was detonated the following month at the Cambridge University football ground, can now see what the motive was. The enemy has been identified. It is not a tiny handful of obstinate politicians who were blocking private members' bills about extending the franchise. It is *all* men, or at the very least the 80 per cent of them who, when they are not engaged in the white slave trade, are indiscriminately spreading gonorrhoea to innocent women.

What do men like doing to relax when they are not destroying the race or corrupting innocent children in this way? Well, they like nothing better than to watch racing, play cricket or spend an afternoon on the golf course. Sabotaging those locations will hit them where it hurts. This, at least, was the rationale behind the destruction of sports facilities which was carried out over the next year or so.

A number of attacks in retaliation for the imprisonment of Emmeline Pankhurst for her role in inciting terrorism were swiftly undertaken. One of the first was in Scotland. In the early hours of 5 April, the grandstand at Ayr racecourse was completely destroyed by fire. This was one of the most costly incidents to date, the value of the grandstand being estimated at £2,000 (perhaps £160,000 in today's terms). An attempt was also made to fire the grandstand at Kelso. Once again, men's sporting activities were seen as being the logical focus for outrage.

Before the fire at Ayr, two other attacks had followed the sentence delivered at the Old Bailey, both at a more conventional terrorist target – the transport system. On the very night that Mrs Pankhurst was convicted, a bomb ripped apart a stationary train near Manchester. It exploded as another train was passing and the driver had a very narrow escape, when a piece of wood flew through the cab of his engine, knocking off his cap.

At 6.15 am on 4 April, the day after the Old Bailey trial ended, a porter arrived for work at Oxted Railway Station in Surrey. He found that a bomb had exploded during the night in the men's lavatory. The doors and windows had been blown out, but the damage could have been a lot worse. Firelighters and a two-gallon can of petrol had been placed near the bomb and the obvious hope of the terrorists was that the explosion would spread burning petrol around and destroy the station entirely. It would not have been the first station to be burned down by the suffragettes. The previous month two other stations, Saunderton and Croxley Green, were burned to the ground. There was no doubt as to who was responsible for these acts. At Saunderton, placards were found propped against a nearby wall with the slogans: 'Votes for Women' and 'Burning to get the Vote'.

The bomb at Oxted had been more sophisticated than the one that went off at Walton-on-the-Hill. Instead of a burning candle, the trigger for this device was a clockwork mechanism and battery. A loaded pistol was also found nearby. Despite the fact that no suffragette literature was left near the scene, as was common practice in attacks of this sort, it was clear that the WSPU were behind the bomb. A piece of paper recovered from the box containing the firelighters was traced to a member of the WSPU living in the London district of Battersea, but she herself had an alibi for the night.

Striking at railways has always been a popular tactic for terrorists. Attacks on them create inconvenience to travellers and so draw attention to the cause in whose name they have been carried out. The disruption can give rise to the feeling that the government is not really in control of the situation. After the fires at Saunderton and Croxley Green and the explosion at Oxted, patrols were instigated to check railway lines and stations regularly for bombs. There was a real fear, justified by other actions of the suffragettes that attempts might be made to derail a train or otherwise cause an accident. On 17 December 1912, the railway signals at Potter's Bar had been tied together and disabled. A note was found, which said, 'The vote is the only remedy'.

While it is sometimes suggested that the suffragettes were very careful to avoid injury to others and that their attacks only harmed property, several statements made by the WSPU at the time undermine this. As early as 1909 for instance, Jenny Baines, who was responsible for trying to burn down the crowded theatre in Dublin, made a public statement when the Prime Minister was giving a speech at

Bingley Hall in Birmingham. She said, 'We warn every citizen attending the meeting in Bingley Hall to beware. He may not only get crippled, he may lose his life eventually'. Nor was she joking. This paid organiser of the WSPU climbed onto a nearby roof with a couple of companions and then used an axe to chop slates off, hurling them at the people below. A police officer was seriously injured.

On the night of 3 April 1913, the day Emmeline Pankhurst was sent to prison for three years, the leaders of the WSPU were even more explicit in their threats. They promised, 'a reign of terror' and announced that what was to be done 'Would stagger humanity'. Even more ominously, one of the women speaking at the headquarters in Kingsway announced that 'human life, we have resolved, will be respected no longer'. This all seems plain enough and, when combined with the actions of the WSPU, no one would be in doubt that some were not at all concerned about causing injury or death.

The fact that some suffragettes were planting bombs to explode near passing trains and sabotaging the signals on busy railway lines makes it hard for us to believe that all members of the WSPU were trying to avoid hurting anybody. This claim is any case a fairly recent one. Meddling with signals and blowing up stations and trains is very hard to square with such a supposed doctrine on the part of the terrorists. If the incidents at which we have just been looking are dubious from this point of view, then the events of 14 April remove all doubt that certain elements among the suffragettes were quite willing to cause injury or death.

At 3.00 pm on the afternoon of Monday, 14 April 1913, a young street urchin in central London noticed smoke billowing out from an object attached to the railings surrounding the Bank of England. He drew this to the attention of a police officer and the constable found that a metal milk can had been fixed to the railings near the Bank of England's Bartholomew Lane entrance. He wrenched it free and ran to the nearby Royal Exchange, outside of which was a fountain. The brave and resourceful man then plunged the mysterious object into the water.

The can turned out to contain an explosive charge, which was to be detonated by a timing device made from a wristwatch and battery. For some reason, the fuse caught fire, but the main charge did not go off. Considering the location of the bomb, immediately opposite the entrance to the Stock Exchange on a busy street in the heart of

London's commercial district, this was fortunate. An explosion could not have failed to cause casualties. There was no direct evidence to link the Bank of England bomb to the WSPU, but it had been attached to the railings with the help of hat pins. As we saw earlier, the finding of hat pins or hairpins was itself a clue to the provenance of a bomb at this time.

One of the most vexing aspects of the suffragette campaign from the point of view of the Liberal government was the way in which they were constantly being manoeuvred, often against their wishes, into taking actions which appeared to be hideously illiberal. Denying half of adult citizens the vote, force-feeding, trying to prevent publication of a newspaper like *The Suffragette*, which criticised the government – these all ran counter to both the Liberal, with a capital 'L', and liberal, with a small 'l', tradition.

The next step taken by Asquith's government continued this trend. It was a ban on open air meetings of the WSPU in London. Home Secretary McKenna directed Sir Edward Henry, who was the Commissioner of Police for the Metropolis, to tackle what he saw as the problem of suffragette rallies in the capital. It was true that recent meetings at Hyde Park and Wimbledon Common had been the target of counter demonstrations, but this was not the main reason for the ban. It was part of a calculated plan to suppress the Women's Social and Political Union and prevent them from appearing in public.

Superintendent Quinn, of Scotland Yard's Special Branch, delivered by hand to Harriet Kerr, acting secretary of the WSPU, the following notice on 15 April:

> It has been brought to the notice of the Secretary of State that the meetings held by the Women's Social and Political Union in Hyde Park, Wimbledon Common and other public open spaces in the Metropolitan area have been the occasion of grave disorder, notwithstanding the presence of large forces of police, and I have advised him that, having regard to the character of the speeches delivered thereat, it is not practicable by any police arrangements to obviate the possibility of similar disorder occurring if such meetings are held.
>
> In these circumstances and in view of the fact that it is the avowed policy of the Women's Social and Political Union to advocate the commission of crimes, the Secretary of State for the Home Department has directed me to instruct the Metropolitan Police to take such steps as are necessary and within their powers to prevent such meetings being held.

The notice was signed by Sir Edward Henry. This was a very ill-judged move by the Home Secretary, because although the Pankhursts and the WSPU had fallen out with both the Labour Party and the more moderate suffragists, nobody liked to see free speech curtailed in this way. Over the next year, not only the WSPU but other groups also sought to defy this ban on open air meetings about women's suffrage.

On the night of Thursday, 17 April, a bomb was found at Aberdeen Railway Station. It was of the same type used at Lloyd George's house and consisted of a charge of gunpowder with a burning candle as the fuse. A railway porter put out the candle before it was able to set off the bomb. A week later, the suffragettes had more success with a larger bomb, which did explode.

In Newcastle-upon-Tyne, the Assize court, forerunner of our Crown Court, was housed in the old Moot Hall, along with the administrative offices of the Northumberland County Council. Just after dusk on 24 April, the caretaker of the building saw two women emerging from an alleyway at the side of the building. He asked them what they were doing, but they both ran off. When Charles Smith, the caretaker, went into the alleyway, he found a string stretched across it, with a card hanging from the string. It bore the words, 'Beware dangerous bomb – run for your life'. This was no idle boast, because at that moment, there was a deafening explosion, as a two-foot-long metal pipe, packed with explosives, went off not far from where he was standing. Windows were shattered, the office of the County Surveyor was wrecked and, so powerful was the blast, the chimney of a neighbouring building was blown down.

These were not the only incidents in April. Killarney golf pavilion in Ireland and Perthshire Cricket Club's pavilion were both burned to the ground, and many letters were damaged in Doncaster. This was in addition to the burning of a number of country houses. A further case of arson that month indicated yet another target towards which the WSPU militants were planning to direct their malice.

Sporting venues were already seen as fair game because they were primarily patronised by men. Men ran the football clubs and golf courses; they also arranged all the horse racing. Emmeline Pankhurst boasted that the damage to golf courses aroused more indignation than any other suffragette activity. There was another area of public life, though dominated by men, and an integral part of the British establishment that the suffragettes had not yet attacked.

During Mrs Pankhurst's trial in early April, two unoccupied houses in Hampstead Garden Suburb were set on fire. A fire was also started in a church, although the police arrived and soon extinguished it. This was a portent of things to come. The suffragettes had decided that the time had come to call the Church of England to account for its lack of support and, in some cases, downright opposition to the campaign for women's suffrage. One point of contention was the insistence of the Anglicans in retaining that part of the marriage vow in which brides promise to 'obey' their new husbands.

Because it is an established church, the Church of England is actually a part of the state in this country. The Head of State is also Head of the Church and so the church is, to a great extent, identified with the actions of the state. The well-known description of the Anglican Church as 'The Conservative Party at prayer' was coined by a suffragette, Agnes Maude Royden. It more or less sums up the attitude of many members of the WSPU in the years leading up to the First World War. For them, the Church of England represented reactionary views and an unwillingness to change. Worse, it was a manifestation of the patriarchy and dominated entirely by men. It did not help that a number of churchmen had opposed the very notion of votes for women and attempted to prove by Biblical exegesis that the Deity Himself did not wish for women to have the parliamentary vote.

All of this, at least as far as the militants were concerned, made Anglican churches bastions of male privilege every bit as unacceptable as the golf courses and cricket grounds that they were trying to put out of action. The fire at the church in Hampstead Garden Suburb was a small one, but churches were soon to become major targets of bombing and arson.

The final bomb of April 1913 exploded in Manchester. This bomb was planted at the city's Free Trade Hall. It was here in 1905 that the very first suffragette act of militancy had taken place, when Christabel Pankhurst and Annie Kenney heckled Edward Grey and Winston Churchill. It can hardly have been a coincidence that the very platform on which the two men had been speaking at that time was destroyed by an explosion on 24 April 1913.

It is not possible to provide a comprehensive list of every bomb attack and act of arson carried out by the suffragettes in March and April of 1913, as there were simply too many of them. Suffice to say that mansions were burned to the ground in Hertfordshire and Norfolk; there was a plot to blow up the grandstand at Crystal Palace football ground; telegraph wires between Grimsby and Immingham in Lincolnshire were cut; and the burning of a train in Teddington and of a second church took place; the list goes on and on.

No responsible government can allow a band of terrorists to rampage across the country unchecked. Regardless of the justice of the demands, constant violence in the form of fires, explosions and other damage to property tends to make governments look weak and ineffectual. For reasons outlined in Chapter 2, looking weak was the last thing that Asquith's administration could afford to do at this time. By the end of April, the decision had been taken at the Home Office that a crackdown would need to take place on the WSPU. A raid was accordingly planned for the end of the month. This operation was successful in that it netted all those leaders of the WSPU whom the government wished to place on trial, but it failed to bring an end to the terrorism. If anything, the pace quickened after the suffragette leaders were behind bars. The WSPU seemed to be like a hydra, and as fast as one head was removed, another sprouted.

Before looking at the raid which was to take place on the headquarters of the WSPU on the last day of April 1913, perhaps we should pause for a moment and ask ourselves a few questions about the motivation of those who were starting the fires and planting the bombs, as well as of the leaders who were inciting, encouraging and financing them. Did they really believe that their militancy could deliver the parliamentary vote to women or could there also have been other reasons for their behaviour?

There were probably a number of explanations for the increasing number of terrorist attacks carried out by WSPU members in 1913 and 1914. For one thing, the vandalism and arson had caused many members to leave and discouraged new ones from joining. In 1909/1910, there were around 4,500 new applications for membership; this had dropped to fewer than 1,000 in the year 1912/1913. At the same time, the number of women joining the National Union of Women's Suffrage Societies was soaring. Many married women left the WSPU at this time and those who remained tended to be single young women, more ready to become involved in illegal activity.

There were also older women, of course; some, like Emily Davison, had little going on in their lives apart from their suffragette activism. For them and also for many younger women, the WSPU functioned as a substitute family, an all-female environment very different from the day to day lives they might otherwise expect to be leading. Life could be pretty dull for women in Edwardian Britain and the militancy offered the chance for excitement, adventure and travel. They could get up to all sorts of daring exploits, even crossing swords with the police and it was all in a good cause! A number of suffragettes, including Annie Kenney, admitted to feeling bored during the 'truce' of 1911 and glad when it ended and they could get back to smashing windows and setting fire to things.

It is quite possible to get a taste for violence and danger; one can almost become addicted to it. If this happens, then life can seem flat and uninteresting in the absence of thrills. After a while, the violence becomes an end in itself and the original motive can be forgotten. We see this happening in modern football hooliganism, for example, and the same thing occurs during terrorist ceasefires. The terrorists become restless and eager to get back to the serious business of planting bombs.

There is no doubt that women who acquired a taste for violence and destruction could be found in the WSPU. These women found their ordinary lives lacking in the excitement they found in militant actions. Such a one was Jennie Baines who, it will be recalled, was among the paid organisers of the WSPU who tried to burn down the Theatre Royal when it was full of people. Her career with the WSPU is almost a case study in the kind of person who picks up a taste for violence.

Sarah Jane Baines, known as Jennie, was almost 40 when she was first involved in militant action with the WSPU. She was present at the Manchester Free Trade Hall in 1905 when Christabel Pankhurst and Annie Kenney were arrested after hitting a policeman. In 1908, she was the first suffragette to be tried by a jury on a charge of unlawful assembly. The following year she was on the roof of a building in Birmingham, throwing slates down at the police and causing injuries to several people. In 1912, Jennie Baines was in Dublin, where she was involved in the arson and bombing at the theatre where Asquith was due to speak. The following year, she was living in the North of England. On 8 July 1913, a bomb exploded in a railway carriage in a siding at Newton Heath. Jennie Baines was arrested and charged with this offence, but jumped bail and went to Australia.

Here was a woman who, at the age of 47, was still committing acts of violence. This lifestyle gave her an identity. So enjoyable did she find breaking windows, starting fires and setting off bombs, that she was unable to break the habit, despite being imprisoned on a number of occasions. There is a strong suspicion that she was involved in many other attacks for which she was not caught. Fires and explosions certainly seemed to follow Jennie Baines and then cease whenever she moved to another district. Writing in *Votes for Women*, Judith Smart says that Baines, 'remembered the suffragette years as her peak experience, when life seemed to take on shape and meaning and an enduring, exalted significance'. This perhaps sums up accurately the feelings of many of the women conducting the guerrilla warfare at that time.

It was not only the women carrying out the attacks who felt this, 'exalted significance', which perhaps their lives had previously been lacking. This satisfaction may have been, at least in the case of some of the most important leaders of the WSPU, more important than the cause itself. Christabel Pankhurst, for instance, was open about the fact that she revelled in the terrorism which she had instigated and now controlled from the safety of her home in Paris. Emmeline Pethick-Lawrence, who fell out with the WSPU over this very question, wrote later that Christabel, 'never made any secret of the fact that to her the means were even more important than the end'. For Christabel Pankhurst, and perhaps to a lesser extent her mother, the militancy was significant in itself, regardless of whether or not it achieved or retarded its stated aim. There was a nobility about the guerrilla warfare being waged in Britain, which had a spiritual significance for women.

It is revealing to read what Christabel Pankhurst herself had to say about the terrorist campaign. On 29 May 1914, she wrote in *The Suffragette*: 'The Militants will rejoice when victory comes in the shape of the vote, and yet, mixed with their joy will be regret that the most glorious chapter in women's history is closed and the militant fight over – over, while so many have not yet known the exultation, the rapture of battle'. Did she really believe that the churches which were being burned down on her instructions, the bombs exploding in public places, the injuries caused by placing dangerous chemicals in post-boxes, that this was really 'the most glorious chapter in women's history'? Did she honestly 'exult' in all this? What kind of person would 'regret' the end of terrorist attacks?

There is another factor that should not be neglected when asking ourselves about the motive for the increasingly frequent explosions and fires for which the WSPU were responsible at this time. Documents seized by the police and read out at court proceedings indicated that the organisation was awash with money. This came not from the shilling membership fee paid by new members, but was rather given by a number of rich supporters, some of whom had pledged over £1,000 each year. The more violent the actions of the suffragettes, the more money that was given by such people. The WSPU might have been shrinking in 1913 from the point of view of membership numbers and popular support, but as far as the paid staff were concerned, they were enjoying an unprecedented boom in 1913 and 1914. Put bluntly, the leaders and organisers of the WSPU were doing very nicely out of this new prosperity.

Many women working in factories and mills were earning less than £1 a week at this time. By contrast, organisers at the WSPU were being paid £2, £3, £4 or even, in the case of Christabel Pankhurst, £10 a week. Annie Kenney, who had left school at the age of 13 to work 12 hours a day in a mill, found herself earning four guineas a week by 1913 – four times as much as the average worker.

Some idea of the lifestyles being led by people like Christabel Pankhurst and Annie Kenney may be gauged by the accounts that they subsequently gave of their lives at this time. By March, 1912, Christabel had left England and gone to live in Paris. From there, she directed the operations of the WSPU, by appointing her friend Annie Kenney to run the organisation in her absence. Kenney travelled to Paris every week to receive her instructions. When she first visited Christabel in Paris, Annie Kenney was rather overawed to be received at the salon of Princesse de Polignac, a friend of Christabel's.

For the whole of the two and a half years that Christabel Pankhurst lived in Paris she did no work at all. All her living expenses were being met by the WSPU. These expenses included an apartment at 8 Avenue de la Grande Armee in the centre of Paris and only a hundred yards or so from the Arc de Triomphe. While other members of the WSPU were on hunger strike and being forcibly fed in Holloway Prison, Christabel Pankhurst was living the life of a well-off lady in the heart of Paris, hobnobbing with princesses.

This state of affairs, with the Pankhursts and their associates living very comfortably on salaries that the ordinary working man or woman could not aspire to, could be prolonged only by escalating the violence. Conversely, the funds might start to dry up if the terrorism died down, as indeed they did during the 1911 truce. This does not, of course, mean that these women were solely in it for the money, but calculations of this sort must have occurred to them.

A glance at the accounts of the WSPU would be enough to warn them of the potential ill effects of scaling back the violence. There was a direct correlation between the levels of militancy and the amount of cash flowing into the coffers of the WSPU. In the year 1907/1908, the annual income was just £7,545. The following year, as things hotted up, this had tripled to £21,213. The following year, 1909/1910, it had shot up to £33,027. It was very clear that the more violent and aggressive the actions of the suffragettes, the more money wealthy people would send their way. Most significantly, in 1910/1911, the period covered by the so-called 'truce', when militancy was abandoned, the income of the WSPU began for the first time to fall, to £29,000. The message was plain, increasing violence brought in money and peaceful methods meant a drop in income.

It would be interesting to know more about the motivations of these wealthy backers, who apparently had an interest in fomenting terrorism in this way. In May 1913, following the arrest of the leadership of the WSPU, the police stated that they had seized a list of subscribers to the WSPU funds. It was said that it would create a sensation if the names on this list were to be published. The implication was that in addition to those who genuinely supported the aims of the WSPU, there were others who had more sinister motives for stirring up violence and unrest.

The Home Office was certainly on the trail of the people financing the terrorists. Plans were mooted for pursuing those who had been giving large amounts and even making it a criminal offence to give money to the WSPU in this way. In fact, shortly before the outbreak of war in 1914, it was explicitly stated by the Home Secretary that moves were afoot to take both civil and criminal proceedings against the people who were bankrolling the WSPU.

Chapter Seven

The Terrorist Campaign Gathers Pace

❝ Have we your sympathy? If not, beware!
Votes for Women! ❞

(Note addressed to members of Haslemere Urban District Council,
included with a bomb left at Haslemere Station in 1913)

Since members of the Women's Social and Political Union had begun to commit acts of vandalism and arson, the government had acted against various individuals on a case-by-case basis. Those caught in the act of starting fires had been prosecuted, as had others like Emmeline Pankhurst, who had merely been encouraging violence. If Asquith and his cabinet had hoped that this would put an end to the burning down of buildings and planting of bombs, then the events of April 1913 would have proved them quite wrong. Acts of terrorism had increased greatly since Mrs Pankhurst's trial at the beginning of the month. The Home Secretary and Prime Minister now decided that a more radical approach should be taken. Rather than arresting this person or that, an attempt should be made to close down the Women's Social and Political Union altogether and prevent the publication of their newspaper, *The Suffragette.*

The morning of Wednesday, 30 April 1913, was just another day in the headquarters of the WSPU. It was a busy place, occupying four floors of Lincoln's Inn House, an imposing building in central London, which still stands today. The WSPU had plenty of money and no expense had been spared in employing staff to type letters, answer telephones and generally carry out the day to day running of the organisation. It was just another working day, with nothing to warn anyone in the building of what was about to occur.

At 11.30 am, a fleet of taxis pulled up outside Lincoln's Inn House and from them leapt 45 plain clothes policemen from Scotland Yard. At the same moment, a large contingent of uniformed officers, who had been hiding in a side street, emerged and the combined force stormed the building. The raid was brilliantly executed. Ten detectives secured each floor and took control at once of the telephones to ensure that no warning was passed to any other members of the WSPU. The office staff were allowed to leave and the leaders who were present were all arrested on charges of conspiring to cause malicious damage. Among those present in the building but not arrested, were Mary Leigh and Gladys Evans, both of whom had been involved in the attempt to burn down the Theatre Royal in Dublin the previous year. Later that day, a removal van pulled up and every document in the place was removed.

At the same time that the raid on the suffragette headquarters was taking place, police descended upon the premises of the Victoria House Press, who had only that week agreed to start printing *The Suffragette.* The previous printer had become too nervous to continue, fearing action of this very sort. The police confiscated the type that had been set, ready to print the next edition of the newspaper, and two days later they arrested the manager of the printing works. While the raids were taking place at Lincoln's Inn House and the printer's, Annie Kenney's flat was also searched.

On Friday, 2 May Annie Kenney, who had been visiting Christabel Pankhurst in Paris, was arrested when she returned to England. In the absence of the Pankhursts, Kenney was in charge of the WSPU. By the end of the week, the chief organiser of the WSPU, its secretary, financial secretary, the assistant editor of *The Suffragette* and several other people were all under lock and key. The offices had been ransacked, all their records removed and their newspaper closed down. It must have seemed to the police and the Home Secretary that it was a good day's work. There was every chance that by removing the entire leadership in this way, they had effectively put an end to the WSPU and that the violence would now stop.

When the women who had been arrested at the WSPU headquarters appeared at Bow Street court, there was an indication of the seriousness with which the case was viewed by the authorities. The Director of Public Prosecutions himself was present at the hearing before the magistrate to state the case for the prosecution. All of those charged in connection with causing malicious damage were remanded in custody. There was also a man in the dock, analytical chemist Edwy Clayton, whose role turned out to be an interesting one. He had been advising Annie Kenney, the acting leader of the WSPU, on explosives and suitable targets for attack. He too was refused bail. Any hope that the terrorist attacks would now end were to be dashed that very afternoon.

The police were keenly aware that attempts would probably be made to show that the suffragettes were not crushed by the latest action against their leaders. On the afternoon of 2 May, a policeman patrolling Piccadilly Circus tube station in London's West End noticed a brown paper bag propped against the wall on one of the platforms. It contained a large bottle, labelled 'Nitroglycerine'. The station was evacuated and Home Office chemists later confirmed that it did indeed contain the explosive. Nitroglycerine is a notoriously unstable explosive, which can be detonated by something as trifling as a sharp blow. Had the bottle been knocked over or accidentally broken, the consequences on a crowded platform would have been extremely serious.

The police had found plenty of evidence during their raid that the leaders of the WSPU were coordinating the arson and bombings. Some of what they found at Lincoln's Inn House was damning. In Annie Kenney's office, for example, a satchel contained eight bottles of benzine, a highly inflammable liquid. At her flat in Mecklenburgh Square, letters were found from Edwy Clayton, suggesting buildings and woodyards which could be burned and giving explicit details as to how this might be done. The National Health Insurance Commission was mentioned in one letter and the suggestion made that someone might visit it during the day, when the building was occupied and then, 'pour out some inflammable liquid, such as benzoline, methylated spirits or paraffin, apply a light and instantly walk out of the building'. In other words, torch offices which contained many ordinary clerks while they were working in the building. Other letters by Edwy Clayton contained cryptic references to mixing up chemicals which would be useful to the suffragette bombers and arsonists. We shall see later to what this may have referred.

One of the most destructive fires ever started by the suffragettes took hold in Bradford on the night of 2 May. The freight sheds of the Midland Railway were burned, causing over £100,000 of damage. This would run into millions at today's values. The sheds were 750 feet long and contained freight cars loaded with carpets and dry goods. The fire brigade only brought the blaze under control by flooding the whole place, in the process damaging many of the goods which had survived the fire.

The WSPU appeared to have access to a steady supply of explosives, both gunpowder and the more dangerous nitroglycerine. Staff at the post office in Borough High Street, just south of London Bridge Station, were sorting parcels on Monday, 5 May, when one caught their attention because it was so heavy and rattled curiously when shaken. The parcel was taken to the nearby police station, where officers opened it. To their horror, they found not only a substantial quantity of gunpowder and lead shot, but most alarmingly, a tube of nitroglycerine. While the militants were raising awareness of women's suffrage by their dangerous antics on the streets, which while attracting attention, also promoted hostility, a move was afoot in parliament to introduce a women's suffrage bill. There was little chance of this reaching the statute book, but the reaction to the bill in the Commons would provide some measure of how the question was being viewed by both the government and the opposition.

It was a Liberal MP who introduced the private bill for women's suffrage. Willoughby Dickinson had been promised by Asquith that if his bill won a second reading in the Commons, then the government would allow it as much time as necessary for it to become law. Dickinson's bill provided for women over 25 who were either householders or married to householders to be given the vote. This would have had the effect of increasing the electorate by six million at one stroke, the biggest jump in the number of people able to vote in this country ever seen. For that reason alone, it was viewed with caution. The British tradition was to increase enfranchisement by small increments.

The House of Commons had in the past given second readings to bills for women's suffrage by healthy majorities in the years preceding Dickinson's, although none had progressed further. It was a sign of the times that this bill did not even make it that far. The Prime Minister spoke against the bill and Foreign Secretary Edward Grey supported it. That the Liberals were generally in favour of female suffrage could be seen by the fact that when it came to the vote, 146 voted in favour of the bill, with 74 against. Overall though, the figures in the House were 268 against and 221 for.

The day after the defeat of Dickinson's bill, on Wednesday, 7 May, a number of newspapers analysed the reasons for its failure. The editorial in *The Times* was typical of many and cut to the heart of the matter. Among other things, it stated:

> *The band of women and girls who call themselves militant suffragettes have done their own cause more harm than they know. The embarrassment they have inflicted on their best friends has been growing more evident of late, and no attempt to conceal it was made in the House of Commons. It lay like a dead weight over the whole course of the debate on the bill.*

The message from *The Times* and other newspapers and magazines was clear: the suffragettes had put back the cause of women's suffrage and were alone responsible for a decline in support for the idea of giving women the vote. The editorial continued, 'But if they have not altogether lost the faculty of reasoning, they must perceive that the attention that they are attracting is more and more positively and angrily hostile, and that the effect on the legislature, which alone can give them what they demand, is to throw back their cause'.

It is true that *The Times* was not sympathetic to women's suffrage, but they had put their finger on the problem here. Previous bills intended to provide for the enfranchisement of women had passed to their second readings with reasonable, even large, majorities. By the summer of 1913, the tide had turned and parliament was reflecting the mood of men and women in the street by rejecting the idea. This change in mood had been brought about almost single-handedly by the violent activities of the WSPU.

Even the pro-suffrage *Manchester Guardian* acknowledged that the suffragettes were responsible for the erosion of support for the cause of women's suffrage. On 6 May, their editorial said:

Though reason, good sense, Liberal tradition, and every consideration to be drawn from a broad view of the march of civilisation are behind Mr Dickinson's bill, there is little prospect of its success in the highly charged state of the political atmosphere. The agitation, therefore, will go on, and we still have to deal with the situation produced by the outrages of the militants. It is the first duty of every government to maintain order.

Both sympathisers and enemies were agreed – the suffragettes' activities were harming and bringing into disrepute the whole idea of women's suffrage.

On the same day that Dickinson's bill failed to gain a second reading, St Catherine's Anglican Church in Hatcham was burned to the ground. The cost of rebuilding the church was estimated at somewhere in the region of £20,000. The suggestion was sometimes made that the WSPU leadership employed dupes to carry out their attacks, foolish people who did not fully understand the nature of what they had become involved in. A possible example of this occurred on the same day that St Catherine's Church was burned down.

Police Constable 728A was on the beat in Northumberland Avenue, near London's Charing Cross Station, when he saw a woman well known to local officers. She was Ada Ward, a middle-aged drunkard who had been arrested many times for being intoxicated in public. It was 2.30 am and there were few people about. He watched curiously as she passed the Grand Hotel and stooped, placing something on the steps of the hotel. He went to investigate and found a metal canister with a lit fuse protruding from it. Attached to the side was a card, bearing the inscription, 'Votes for Women'. The constable extinguished the fuse and then picked up the bomb and placed it on a traffic island in the road. Then he went in pursuit of Ada Ward. When he found her, she denied having been near the Grand Hotel and PC 728A took her back there, only to find that the bomb had been removed by somebody.

When Ward was brought to court the following day on a charge of being a suspected person, both the magistrate and the solicitor acting for the police drew the same conclusion about the vanishing bomb. Mr Dickinson, the magistrate, said that it seemed to him that somebody must have been watching Ada Ward and that she was hardly the sort of woman one would expect to be involved in political activism of this sort. In the end, Ada Ward was remanded in custody so that the police could make further enquiries. That night, the terrorists turned their attention to another church, possibly the most famous in the entire country.

Having decided that the Anglican Church was an appropriate target for their anger, the WSPU must have thought that there was no reason to fiddle around with little parish churches. Why not strike a blow at the very heart of this establishment proxy? On the morning of 7 May, a verger at St Paul's Cathedral in London was passing the bishop's throne, when he heard a loud ticking. He traced the source of the noise to a brown paper parcel which had been hidden beneath a chair in the choir. The verger plunged the parcel into a bucket of water and called the police. When they undid it, they found that the parcel contained a bomb, which was to have been detonated by a clock and two batteries. The police later described the device as, 'small, but fiendishly powerful'. An interesting circumstance was that the explosive used in this bomb was not gunpowder or dynamite, but the far more dangerous nitroglycerine.

Nitroglycerine is liable to explode when banged or splashed. For that reason, it had since the 1860s been used in the form of dynamite, which consists of nitroglycerine that has been absorbed by a form of porous clay called kieselguhr. It is easy enough to manufacture nitroglycerine in a laboratory, or even at home, but there are two chief difficulties with making nitroglycerine – one is the amount of heat generated by the process and the other is ensuring that the proportions are precisely correct. Failing to take into account either of these factors can result in the substance exploding during manufacture.

During the raid on the WSPU headquarters, a letter was found from the analytical chemist Edwy Clayton, in which he referred specifically to the problem with getting the quantities right for some substance he was preparing for the use of the militant suffragettes. In view of the fact that nitroglycerine was only used in a small number of bombs planted in the month following Clayton's arrest, it is reasonable to assume that he had previously made some nitroglycerine and passed it on to the bombers.

That same morning that the bomb was found in St Paul's Cathedral, the cricket pavilion at Bishop's Park in Fulham was burned to the ground and a fire was started at a woodyard in Lambeth. An unoccupied house in Hendon was also set alight by an incendiary device. Close examination of the bombs recovered, which had failed to explode, showed that they had been well-made, but suffered from minor defects such as broken connections in the firing circuits. Some of these related to the soldering of electrical connections, indicating that those using the soldering irons might not have had much experience. It was the ineptitude of the bombers which was responsible for the failure of their devices to go off, not a reluctance to cause explosions in public places.

On 10 May, the suffragette bombers turned once again to men's sport. In perhaps the most bizarre bomb attack ever carried out in this country, the changing rooms at the football ground of Cambridge University were damaged by an explosion. As in similar attacks, cans of petrol and other combustible material was placed near the seat of the explosion, but they had not caught fire. Other bombs were also planted that day, including one at the waiting room at Lime Street Station, in Liverpool. Although not large, it had been surrounded with iron nuts and bolts, obviously to increase the chances of causing injury or damage. The timing mechanism here was primitive – an oil-soaked fuse which had been lit before the bomber made herself scarce. Luckily, it had gone out, but the intention had definitely been to cause an explosion in a busy railway station.

It was apparent that arresting the leadership of the WSPU had had the opposite effect to that intended – rather than a reduction in terrorism the violent attacks seemed to be increasing day by day. Nor was this new wave of bombings limited to England. On the same day that the bombs had been left at the station in Liverpool and the Cambridge football ground, a device was found in a lavatory at the Empire Theatre in Dublin.

During the Saturday afternoon performance at the Empire Theatre, a woman obtained the key to the lavatory from one of the attendants. When she entered, she discovered a bomb made up of 24 cartridges of gunpowder. The fuse was burning. Showing great presence of mind, the woman plunged the bomb into a washbasin full of water. Once again, those lighting the fuse of such a device showed a complete disregard for the safety and welfare of the public.

On the same day, Farington Hall, a country house near Dundee, was destroyed. Fires had been started simultaneously in half a dozen places. Back in England, an alarming development was the sending of explosives through the post. Ticking was heard from a parcel at Reading post office. It was addressed to a municipal official in the town. The police were called and found that the parcel was a time bomb, containing both gunpowder and also a quantity of nitro-glycerine.

The wave of bombings did nothing to help the cause of the suffragettes, who were fast becoming extremely unpopular with the public. Their reputation was hardly enhanced by the evidence produced at the committal proceedings for those arrested during the police raid on Lincoln's Inn House. Before the case was sent to the Old Bailey, preliminary hearings were held at Bow Street Magistrates Court, to establish if a *prima facie* case could be made out against them. They were charged with 'Conspiring together and with others maliciously to cause damage, injury and spoil in and on property belonging to tradesman and others, contrary to the Malicious Damage Act 1861'.

The hearings which took place in May were conducted before Sir Henry Curtis-Bennett, the chief metropolitan magistrate. He made no secret of his feelings about the man – Edwy Clayton – and women in the dock and was soon a figure of hatred for the suffragette movement. When an application for bail was made on behalf of Flora Drummond, on the grounds that her health was bad and that she was suffering from an 'internal complaint', Sir Henry remarked sourly, 'She's suffering from extensive bad behaviour'.

The newspapers reported details of the WSPU's financial arrangements which must have made many people ask what was going on. The sums of money mentioned were so enormous that one wonders what the average working person made of it all. To give just two examples, it was mentioned that a cheque from one of the WSPU's bank accounts had been drawn in favour of Beatrice Saunders, an officer of the organisation, for the sum of £3,706 2/6. There was a good deal of speculation in the press as to what Miss Saunders could have been doing to receive such a huge sum. Working-class women who had paid their shillings to join the WSPU would typically have to have worked for a hundred years to earn this much money!

It is hard to avoid the suspicion that information like this was being produced in court because it was precisely the kind of thing that the newspapers would pick up on. There was no suggestion that any of the figures being bandied about during the hearings at Bow Street were untrue. At any rate, neither the women in the dock nor their lawyers challenged any of it.

Another titbit that found its way into the papers was that Christabel Pankhurst, who had for over a year been living in Paris, was paid £175 over four months in salary and expenses. This would have worked out at over £500 a year, ten times as much as the average person was earning at that time. What Christabel Pankhurst was spending this salary on, we do not know, though it is possible that some of it went towards entertaining foreign royalty.

Even the minor expenditure of the WSPU was lavish. It was the custom to give members badges and medals for various acts, such as going on hunger strike. According to the papers seized by the police during their raid on the headquarters, £90 had been spent with one firm alone on such trinkets. This represents two or three years' wages for a female textile worker at that time.

If the intention of reading out details of the WSPU's financial dealings in open court was to blacken them in the eyes of the public, then it probably succeeded. So steep was the decline in applications for membership after that month that the WSPU soon stopped publishing the figures. The overall impression was of a bunch of very highly-paid people for whom money was no object.

Another bomb attack was carried out against a sporting target on 12 May and even by the odd standards of the suffragettes, it was a very strange place to plant a bomb. At 5.30 am, George Cook, caretaker of the premises of the Oxted Badminton and Lawn Tennis Club, arrived to work and at once became aware of an ominous ticking when he entered the clubhouse. It was coming from a metal canister with a clockwork mechanism attached to the top. He put it in a fire bucket full of water and then called the police. The bomb turned out to contain nitroglycerine. A card was later found in the grounds of the club, upon which was written, 'Votes for Women'.

Perhaps it was because of the bad publicity that was generated by the committal proceedings, this publicity being encouraged by the magistrate, that some of the suffragettes decided to try and assassinate

Sir Henry Curtis-Bennett. On 14 May, a parcel was sent to him at Bow Street. It aroused the suspicions of staff there and they called the police. The package was an ingenious letter bomb – a tin full of gunpowder had a round of ammunition fixed, so that it pointed at the explosive charge. A nail was held in place over this, with the point resting on the percussion cap of the cartridge. A sharp tap would have been enough to detonate the device.

We tend to think of letter bombs as a weapon of modern terrorists, but actually it was the suffragettes who first devised them. Later on, more sophisticated letter bombs were made, using phosphorous. Lloyd George was the intended recipient of one of these lethal packages.

When the letter bomb failed to kill Sir Henry, more direct methods were adopted. A few days after being sent the lethal package, Sir Henry was walking along the cliffs near Margate, in Kent. Two women walked towards him. He did not realise his danger until one of the women shoved him hard, trying to knock him off balance, and the second then grabbed hold of him and attempted to push him off the top of the cliff. He was very shaken by this experience, after which he was assigned detectives who accompanied him everywhere.

The bomb attacks and arson continued throughout the rest of the month. It would be tedious simply to list these many and various acts of terrorism. Most were relatively minor incidents of fire-raising: the burning of haystacks, wood yards and other locations where a mass of combustible material would make a good blaze. These days, terrorism is far more often associated with guns and explosives than arson, but there is a long tradition in this country of fire being used as a tool of political violence. For angry and discontented people without access to explosives, arson is a very public way of drawing attention to their grievances. During the Swing Riots in 1830, for instance, haystacks were routinely torched in England as a political protest.

The IRA was at one time very fond of using arson as a terrorist weapon. They often tended too, just like the suffragettes, to focus their attention upon commercial premises. In fact, the IRA were so keen on starting fires, particularly in shops, that it seems very likely that they picked up the idea from the suffragettes. We can see this connection very clearly in the first IRA campaign on mainland Britain, which began in 1920, just six years after the suffragette arson campaign came to an end. This terrorist campaign, just like that of the suffragettes a decade earlier, has also largely disappeared from memory.

A small bomb was planted by suffragettes outside the National Gallery in London on 15 May. It failed to go off. The next day, there were other bombs in locations as far apart as a library in south London, a church in Hastings and an hotel in Brentwood. One bomb was aimed again at the railways. Beneath the footbridge at Westbourne Park Station, a package was found which had been placed there with the intention of setting fire to the bridge. It was made of live cartridges, explosives and oil-soaked cotton wool. The fuse had been lit, but later gone out.

As the committal proceedings of the prominent suffragettes facing conspiracy charges continued at Bow Street Magistrates Court, more information was emerging to shed light on the practical consequences of the WSPU's campaign of violence. As already asserted, it is often suggested today that the suffragette militants took great care to harm only property. The burning and destruction of letters is sometimes cited as an example of this – nobody could be hurt by fires taking place in iron pillar boxes. At worst, it would surely cause no more than a little inconvenience to the intended recipients of the letters that were destroyed.

A postman was summoned to give evidence at Bow Street about the injuries he had received from a fire started in a pillar box. It emerged that he and a number of other workers had been burned by fires started by suffragettes in letter boxes. It is intriguing to see how this aspect of the suffragette campaign is now presented by modern historians in a completely different light than it was viewed at the time.

Not all the arson attacks on houses in 1913 were against castles and grand mansions. Some suffragettes were burning down the homes of ordinary people who had nothing at all to do with their cause. On the night of 16 May, Miriam Pratt, a 23-year-old schoolteacher from Norwich, went to Cambridge with two fellow suffragettes and set fire to two houses. There was nothing remarkable about these houses; they were empty because they were being decorated. After breaking into one of the properties in Storey's Way and setting fire to it, they crossed the road and splashed paraffin about in another house and torched that one as well. Miss Pratt had the misfortune to be living with her uncle, who was a police sergeant. When he found out what they had done, he was so horrified that he turned them over to the police in Cambridge. It is evident, therefore, that the activities of the militant suffragettes were not restricted to those whom they saw as their enemies. Anybody at all was fair game, even ordinary householders whose homes were being decorated.

On the day after the houses in Cambridge were burned, came a bomb attack in Scotland. On 17 May, a bomb containing 12 lbs of gunpowder was placed in St Mary's Church at Dalkeith Park. The fuse was lit, but went out. Four days later, the bombers were more successful when they attacked the Royal Observatory in Edinburgh. It is impossible to be sure of the reasons for this – perhaps the fact that the complex of buildings was perched high above the city of Edinburgh on Blackford Hill, and so the sound of the explosion would reverberate across the whole city, that made the observatory seem like a suitable target.

More likely is the fact that there was a precedent for such an action – London's Royal Observatory had suffered a similar attack less than 20 years earlier when 26-year-old Frenchman Martial Bourdin decided that he wished to blow up the observatory at Greenwich. He attempted to do so on 6 February, 1894, but his plans were unfortunately thwarted in the most gruesome way imaginable. His chosen explosive was nitroglycerine and, as he made his way up Greenwich Hill to the Royal Observatory, he must have stumbled and dropped his bomb. Nitroglycerine reacts badly to being shaken or banged and the can full of the oily liquid went off at once. Splashes of blood and fragments of Bourdin's body, including a two-inch-long piece of bone, were found more than 60 yards from the site of the explosion. Over 50 pieces of the unlucky terrorist were later collected from a wide area of Greenwich Park.

Professor Ralph Allen Sampson had been appointed Astronomer Royal for Scotland in 1910. He and his wife lived 'over the shop' in a house next to the building which held the telescopes. At 1.00 am on 21 May, Professor Sampson was woken up by a loud noise, which he took to be a door being slammed somewhere. In the morning, he found that a bomb had gone off inside the main building of the observatory. The terrorists had got in by breaking a pane of glass in an external door and making their way down a spiral staircase to the chronograph room.

None of the telescopes or other scientific instruments were harmed by the bomb, which caused only a certain amount of structural damage, blowing out windows, bringing down a ceiling and chipping brickwork. The clock that drove the 24-inch reflecting telescope was housed in the room where the blast occurred, but had only been covered in plaster. It was still working.

That the suffragettes had been responsible for the bomb outrage was beyond doubt. A woman's handbag was left behind and also some biscuits. Two pieces of paper were also deliberately placed at the scene. One of these said, 'How beggarly appears argument, before defiant deed! Votes for women'. On the other, was written, 'From the beginning of the world every stage of human progress has been from scaffold to scaffold and from stake to stake'.

Incidents like the attack on the observatory in Edinburgh were causing resentment to build up against the suffragettes for the escalating terrorism. Unfortunately, this was manifested in hostility towards even the non-militant suffragists of the NUWSS. It seemed that any mention of female suffrage was now associated with arson and explosions. Even those who had been in favour of women being granted the parliamentary vote were now changing their minds. The entire movement was being tainted by the mad actions of a handful of fanatics. It was becoming hazardous now for any meetings to be held by either suffragettes or suffragists. This was neatly illustrated by the events in the coastal town of Hastings on 20 May 1913.

One of the largest and most important houses in Hastings had been razed to the ground by the suffragettes the previous month. This was Levitsleigh, formerly the home of the town's MP. Many people in Hastings were angry about this act of wanton destruction and it became risky for the local branch of the WSPU to meet in public. The information appearing in the newspapers about the apparently vast amounts of money at the disposal of the suffragettes did nothing to help matters and when on 20 May, the WSPU announced that they would be holding an open air meeting at Wellington Square, there were rumours that a counter demonstration was planned by residents of Hastings, with the intention of showing the suffragettes exactly what people thought about their behaviour. Following the advice of the police, who were naturally keen to avoid a riot, the WSPU cancelled their meeting.

By ill coincidence, there was a meeting that night of the local branch of the National Union of Women's Suffrage Societies, an organisation that rejected militant action in favour of constitutional methods. This was too fine a point for the angry crowds who had gathered to oppose the suffragettes in Wellington Square and so they transferred their attentions to the Suffrage Club in Havelock Street, throwing eggs and stones at the building. When the women tried to leave, they were manhandled and abused. Some took refuge in a nearby hotel, with the result that the crowd smashed the windows. Some witnesses said that there were as many as 3,000 people outside Green's Hotel, baying for the blood of the suffragists.

Similar scenes were enacted a few days later in London, when Sylvia Pankhurst tried to hold a meeting in Victoria Park in the East End of London. The rally was to have been a large one, with 15 wagons for the members of the WSPU and Labour Party to speak from. Many East Enders though had different ideas and the suffragettes were mobbed. The police had to step in and escort the suffragettes to safety. The crowd were angry, not at the idea of equal suffrage but because of the bombs which were going off almost every day. Partly due perhaps to the press coverage of the committal proceedings of the WSPU leadership, the feeling was growing among working-class men and women that these women did not represent people like them at all.

Sylvia Pankhurst's abortive rally in the East End took place on Sunday, 25 May. Two days later came a suffragette attack that was even more irresponsible than usual and which could have had terrible consequences. As the Bristol Express passed through Reading Station on 27 May, a bomb was thrown from a window of the train onto the platform. At the same time, suffragette literature was also thrown from the train. The bomb exploded without causing too much damage, but it was a foolhardy and dangerous action.

Throughout June, the trial took place at the Old Bailey of those arrested during the raid on Lincoln's Inn House. The six women and one man, Edwy Clayton the chemist, were charged with 'conspiring together and with others to inflict damage on property and inciting other members of the WSPU to damage property'. The bombings continued during the trial.

On 11 June, a bomb exploded at the new wing of the post office in Newcastle-on-Tyne. On 15 June, a bomb was found in the waiting room at Eden Park Station, near Beckenham. The clockwork mechanism which had been meant to trigger the device had stopped. Two days later, there was another explosion in central London. At 4.00 pm on Tuesday, 17 June, there was an explosion near Blackfriars Bridge. The bomb had been thrown from the bridge and exploded as it hit the surface of the Thames. A plume of water shot up and a cloud of blue smoke rose into the air. The railway bridge was shaken by the explosion and railway workers rushed to the scene to check that no damage had been done to the bridge. Whoever had thrown the bomb had disappeared.

Although it had not been long in force, the notorious 'Cat and Mouse Act' was already making a nonsense of the law. At the conclusion of the suffragette conspiracy trial, there were a number of prison sentences, including one of a year and nine months for Edwy Clayton. Clayton, it will be remembered, had been suggesting targets for the terrorists and also making explosives for them. Given the evidence, he might very well have thought that a year and nine months imprisonment was a light-enough punishment. In fact, he was freed after just 15 days, having gone on hunger strike. As soon as he was out of prison, he left the country. It was becoming very apparent that there was little point in sending suffragettes and their supporters to prison, because they would be back on the streets in a matter of days.

On the same day as the bomb at Blackfriars Bridge in London, came an attack which could have been catastrophic. On the morning of Wednesday, 18 June, John Sales, who lived near Birmingham, was walking along the towpath of the Stratford-upon-Avon Canal, which runs south of Birmingham. Sales, who lived at Warstock, now a suburb of Birmingham, was horrified to find that the canal bank had almost been breached by what looked like the crater of a very large explosion. At this point, near Alcester Road, the canal runs along some high ground, above fields and farmhouses which lie in a valley below.

On investigating, it was found that a hole five feet wide had been blown in the embankment and that the lip of this crater was only three inches from the edge of the water. A spade lay nearby and also the charred remains of a long fuse. A piece of cardboard was propped up, not far away, on which were the words, 'Votes for women. Mind your canals'. There were no locks for 11 miles on that stretch of the canal and so if the wall had been breached at this high point, then 11 miles of water would have been emptied into the farmland below, with inevitable loss of life. It was a very narrow escape indeed for those living in the cottages beneath the embankment.

There were two more incidents the following weekend, one aimed at a church and the other at a university. Just after dawn on the morning of Saturday, 21 June, fishermen at sea off the coast of St Andrews, on Scotland's east coast, saw smoke rising from the university in the town. They returned to shore and notified the coastguard, who then called the fire brigade. Somebody had broken into the Gatty Marine Laboratory at St Andrews University and spread inflammable liquid about the place. The east wing of the laboratory, which housed many scientific drawings and other materials, was gutted by the fire. This wanton destruction caused a lot of anger in the town against the vandals responsible.

At the other end of the country, in Southend, Essex, an attempt had been made to burn down a local parish church. When the verger entered the church early on Saturday morning, he found that the door to the organ was open, which was unusual. Inside was a collection of live cartridges, oily rags, paper and other inflammable material. A wax taper had been lit and placed so that it would act as a fuse. Fortunately, a draught seemed to have blown it out and saved the church from destruction.

The fire at St Andrews University was one of many such attacks in Scotland, which for a time bore the brunt of the suffragette 'arson squads'. Although many of the fires started caused only minor damage, others threatened life and were hugely costly to either the owners of the properties or the companies which insured them. Two examples from the end of June illustrate this point. Both took place in the early hours of 30 June.

What *The Times* described as 'the most disastrous fire that has occurred in Stirlingshire for many years' broke out at Ballikinrain Castle, a huge country house which contained over a hundred rooms. The fire was started at about 3.00 am and although the fire brigade were called, there was no ready supply of water for them to work with. The entire building was completely destroyed. The fire had been deliberately started and two women cyclists had been seen in the vicinity a few hours earlier, with packages.

At the same time that Ballikinrain Castle was being burned down, the railway station at Leuchars Junction, near St Andrews was also going up in flames. Tins of inflammable material were found near the fire, along with suffragette literature. The combined cost of these two fires alone came, in modern terms, to millions of pounds.

The bomb attacks and arson continued unabated through July 1913. On the night of Saturday, 5 July 1913, a bomb exploded in a passageway beneath Liverpool Cotton Exchange. The Cotton Exchange, an office building erected in 1906, was the centre for the city's cotton trade and was linked to the world by a state-of-the-art system of telegraph and telephone lines. There were no clues, but the bombing was generally attributed to the suffragettes.

The following Wednesday, the wife of a local doctor approached the police and admitted that she was the one who had detonated the bomb. Edith Rigby was well-known to the police, having been arrested a number of times for her actions at protests in Liverpool. When she appeared in court the following day, Mrs Rigby gave as her justification for the bombing, the passing of the 'Cat and Mouse Act'. We catch a glimpse in her speech to the magistrate of the adoration that Emmeline Pankhurst awoke in her followers. She said in court, 'Under this Act, one of the greatest women in the land is going to be done to death ... I do not think the government realises that it is literally going to kill that woman'. The magistrate's response was to remand her until the following Monday. Before she was taken from the dock, Edith Rigby suddenly announced that she wished to claim responsibility for another attack, the destruction by fire of a house belonging to Lord Leverhulme, which had taken place on the Monday after the bomb at the Cotton Exchange. The cost of rebuilding the house had been estimated at some £20,000.

On 8 July, a fire was started at Southport Pier. Fortunately, two fishermen saw the flames and bravely tackled the fire themselves. Empty bottles of paraffin were found and a woman had been seen leaving the scene of the fire shortly before it was discovered.

As already noted, the same names crop up again and again when examining the terrorist actions of the WSPU. Many of these familiar names belong to women who were paid employees of the WSPU, such as those responsible for trying to burn down the theatre in Dublin 1912. Not only were they not thrown out of the WSPU for their actions, but they were still being paid a year later when the police raised the headquarters at Lincoln's Inn House. Indeed, two of them, Mary Leigh and Gladys Evans, were actually present during the raid. The third of the women who so very narrowly avoided committing mass murder on that occasion, Jennie Baines, was also retained by the WSPU as a paid organiser. She had been sent to prison for seven months for her part in the attack on the Theatre Royal, although of course she had not served anything like that, due to going on hunger strike. Her experiences in Dublin seem to have taught her nothing, because in July 1913, she was on trial again, in connection with explosives and firearms.

Jennie Baines was a classic example of the sort of woman who has to have a cause to which she might devote her life. She had been a member of the Salvation Army, a temperance advocate and other things besides, when she joined the WSPU. She was in and out of prison for the next few years, being implicated in various arson attacks. On 10 July 1913, Mrs Baines appeared in court in Manchester with her husband and 16-year-old son, charged with having set fire to two railway carriages at Newton Heath. Also in the dock was Kate Wallwork, secretary of the Manchester branch of the WSPU.

The Newton Heath outrage was another of those cases where it was more by luck than anything else that an innocent person was not killed by the suffragettes' bomb. At about 11.30 pm on 7 July, the night-watchman at Wilson's Brewery saw two men and a woman walking towards the Monsall Road railway sidings. Twenty minutes later, a police constable on his routine patrol walked up the road which ran between the brewery and the railway lines. There was a loud explosion and he was showered with debris, including large pieces of broken glass.

A bomb had been placed in a carriage standing in the sidings and it had gone off, shattering the carriage and starting a fire. At the subsequent court proceedings, the police gave evidence that when the Baines family were arrested, a tin of gunpowder was found, as well as a loaded revolver. Jennie Baines was herself currently out of prison, having been freed under the 'Cat and Mouse Act'. That somebody released in this way, could then go on to commit another act of arson, made the law look ridiculous. She and her family jumped bail and sought refuge in Australia.

On the same day that the carriage was blown up in Newton Heath, the suffragettes attacked an aqueduct, also in Manchester. An inspector called James Blythe was walking along the Brock aqueduct, which ran from Thirlmere, when he noticed something bright and shiny concealed near a crack in the stonework of the aqueduct. This turned out to be a lantern with a candle inside. This led to a fuse, which in turn ran to a bomb, which had been wedged between two stone blocks. The candle, evidently intended to light the fuse, had fallen sideways and gone out. The consequences of damaging an aqueduct in this way could have been very serious.

One of the most remarkable aspects of the suffragette bombing campaign is the extraordinary leniency of the sentences imposed. These were light enough to begin with, seldom more than six months or a year and in reality, most of the women were released within a few weeks when they went on hunger strike.

Two days after Jennie Baines appeared in court, a Welsh suffragette – Margaret Mackworth, of Carleon – was tried on what would today be viewed as a very serious offence: placing an explosive substance in a post office letter box. She was seen placing a package in a pillar box. Almost at once, smoke began billowing from the box, upon which Mackworth was seized by passers-by. When the pillar box was opened, it was found that the package contained two glass tubes, one of which contained phosphorous and the other, a substance that was not named in open court, but only whispered to the magistrate.

It is hard to imagine a bomber of this sort heading anywhere today, other than straight to prison. Rather than being sent to prison, Margaret Mackworth, however, was merely fined £10, with a further £10 to be paid in costs. It was not as though this sort of crime was victimless. On 19 July, six postboxes in Birmingham were set alight by the use of chemicals. A postman taking letters from one box was burned by a corrosive liquid which had been poured into the pillar box by militant suffragettes.

On the same day that the postman in Birmingham was injured, the railways were once again the target for the suffragettes. That evening, a porter at Haslemere Station in Surrey found a box on the stairs leading from one of the platforms. He had the presence of mind to plunge the box into a pail of water, which was fortunate, because it was, of course, a time bomb. When the police later opened it, they found it consisted of a clock, battery, fuse and explosives. There was also a message, addressed to the members of the newly formed Haslemere Urban District Council, which said, 'Have we your sympathy? If not, beware! Votes for women.'

That night, a large house at Selly Oak, near Birmingham, was nearly burned to the ground. Suffragette literature was found nearby. It was a particularly ill-chosen target as, until a few weeks earlier, the house had been used as a home for orphan girls.

Chapter Eight

Winter, 1913

‘ *$1,000,000 Damage and Two Deaths –*
Suffragettes Suspected. ’

(*The New York Times*, 22 December 1913)

By autumn 1913, it was apparent to everybody other than some of the more dedicated members of the WSPU that their activities were not only failing to advance the cause of women's suffrage, but that they were now acting as a positive hindrance. Having dealt with the wave of industrial unrest, known as the Great Unrest, which was itself marked by acts of sabotage, and facing now the threat of armed insurrection in Ireland, the last thing that Asquith's government could afford to do was display any weakness in the face of terrorism or the menace of violence.

Support for the WSPU was falling, while at the same time membership of the moderate National Union of Women's Suffrage Societies was growing by the day. The suffragettes were rapidly becoming an irrelevant distraction in the struggle for female emancipation. They had been reduced to a small, fringe group, a corps of professional activists concerned less with democracy and the views of the majority than seeking to impose their own ideology by the use of violence against those who disagreed with them. Given the circumstances, they had no other weapon in their armoury but the continued use of explosives and petrol.

In the early months of the bombing campaign, many of the bombs planted by the suffragettes had failed to explode. With each new bomb though, the makers were becoming more proficient and from November 1913 onwards, the bombs planted were, more often than not, going off and damaging their intended targets.

On the night of Monday, 10 November, the pavilion at Catford Lawn Tennis Club in south London was burned down by suffragettes. A few hours after this fire, a more serious incident took place in Manchester. At 4.20 am on 11 November, residents living near Alexandra Park in Manchester were woken by a huge explosion. Many people rushed into the street to see what had happened and found that their front gardens were covered with broken glass. An 18-inch-long metal pipe, packed with explosives, had been placed on the steps of a greenhouse in Alexandra Park. The greenhouse contained a valuable collection of cacti. When the bomb had exploded, it had hurled shards of glass across much of the surrounding area.

Three days later, the bombers struck again at the Sefton Park Palm House in Liverpool. This time, the bomb failed to explode. The same month saw a number of attacks – a fire started by suffragettes at Streatham Hill Station in London, the destruction by fire of 'Begbrook', a mansion near Bristol and various other incidents of arson, including the burning of a haystack at Burton on Trent.

December brought fresh attacks. One of the most serious of these took place in Manchester before a visit by Prime Minister Asquith. On 7 December, shortly before the Prime Minister was due to arrive in the city, The Rusholme Exhibition Centre was completely gutted by fire. Suffragette literature was scattered nearby, along with the message, presumably addressed to Asquith, 'This is your welcome to Manchester and Oldham.' At about the same time, an attempt was made to burn down a grandstand at the Aintree racecourse. On 16 December, a fire was started in St Anne's Church in Liverpool's Aigburth district. A lot of damage was caused, the organ and pulpit being destroyed by the flames, although the fabric of the church itself was saved.

Over the course of two days in December, 1913, two separate incidents occurred which indicated just how dangerous the suffragette attacks were becoming. Members of the WSPU had rented and used as their district headquarters a house at 12, Dalmeny Avenue in London. This property backed onto Holloway Prison, where many imprisoned suffragettes were held at various times. It had proved possible to signal to these prisoners from the back windows of the house in Dalmeny Avenue. On the night of Saturday, 13 December, Emmeline Pankhurst was being held in the prison and a suffragette had climbed onto the roof of No. 12 and serenaded her by playing a cornet. Mrs Pankhurst was released a few days later, leaving only one suffragette prisoner in Holloway.

By 18 December 1913, Rachel Pearce, serving 18 months for burning down a mansion in Hampton, was the only suffragette prisoner in Holloway. Pearce had been in prison for a month and was currently being force-fed, after embarking on a hunger strike. There was a good deal of anger among members of the WSPU at her treatment.

On the night of Thursday, 18 December, the London districts of Camden and Holloway were shaken by two tremendous explosions, which shook the area for a mile or so around Holloway Prison. The explosions were separated by a period of 30 seconds. Many houses near Holloway Prison had their windows blown out by the bombs. Investigations showed that two charges of dynamite had been buried at the foot of the wall surrounding the prison garden. This wall was so severely damaged that it would have to be demolished and rebuilt. It could hardly have been a coincidence that the seat of the explosions was directly opposite the back garden of 12 Dalmeny Avenue.

The police found the remains of two 50-foot-long fuses that had been laid from 12 Dalmeny Avenue, all the way to the wall of Holloway Prison. They also found a mass of blonde hair in the garden of No. 12 and also some bloodstains. It looked as though the bomber might have been injured by the explosion she had triggered. The trail led nowhere though and nobody was ever tried for this particular action.

There was considerable anger locally about the bomb attacks. A family living next door to the house that the suffragettes had been renting were especially upset. Two small children at 10 Dalmeny Avenue had been asleep in bed when the dynamite was detonated. Their bedroom window had been blown in and their bed covered with jagged pieces of glass. Miraculously, neither child had been injured.

We come now to what is perhaps the worst attack attributed to the activists of the WSPU. It must be said, however, that it is not certain that this attack, if it was an attack, really was the work of the suffragettes, although that was the general assumption at the time.

Two days after the bomb attack on Holloway Prison, there was a disastrous fire at Portsmouth Dockyard. There were a number of old wooden buildings at the dockyard, in particular a semaphore tower dating from the late eighteenth century. It was thought that the fire began in a sail loft, before spreading to a rigging house and then the semaphore tower. Various stores and oil tanks caught fire and the blaze was so fierce that the battleship *Queen Mary*, which was moored nearby, had to be towed to safety. When the flames had been extinguished, it was found that two sailors had died. The cost of the damage caused was estimated to be in the region of £200,000. Almost immediately, rumours began to circulate that this fire had been started deliberately by the suffragettes.

When the police raided the Kingsway headquarters of the WSPU at the end of April 1913, they seized a large quantity of paperwork, including correspondence. One letter excited their special interest. It was addressed to Flora Drummond, a prominent organiser for the WSPU, and signed by a code name. Judging by the contents, the sender of this letter had been in touch with the WSPU before. In light of what happened at Portsmouth that December, this communication could have been very significant. It read:

I am very sorry that I have not been able to reply to your letter before now, but I have only just returned from a short stay at Hove. I did not get your letter until yesterday. With regard to the proposal you make therein, it

must be obvious that the sum you mentioned is really insignificant com-
pared to the splendid result to our cause if the job comes off all right. It
will cost not less than £20, besides two men. Although I would love to be
the sole villain of the piece, I fear the dockyard police would suspect a lady
visitor, and so I propose to be the brains this time and not the hands. At
any rate, the damage would not be less than £20,000.

There are a number of interesting points about this letter which could
tie in very neatly with the Portsmouth fire – the mention of the dockyard police tells us that an illegal action was planned in connection
with a dockyard. The fact that this action was likely to cause over
£20,000 worth of damage, tells us that a fire is being contemplated.
Hove, like Portsmouth, is on the south coast of England, which raises
the possibility that the dockyard discussed in this letter is in fact
Portsmouth.

It certainly appears from the letter quoted above that the leadership
of the WSPU were in negotiations with somebody in 1913 who was
offering to start a large fire in a dockyard, a dockyard that might well
have been on the south coast. That such a fire actually took place a few
months later might be a coincidence, but if so, it would have been a
very remarkable one. Another hint that the Portsmouth fire might
have been carried out by or on behalf of the WSPU is provided by the
fact that it was mentioned in the next issue of *The Suffragette*. Although
stopping short of claiming that it had been their work, it seems curious
that the writers of the magazine would have said anything about this
deadly blaze, had it been just another accidental fire.

There is no doubt that it was generally assumed at the time that the
suffragettes were responsible for this terrible event. The rumours even
reached across the Atlantic within a few days. On 22 December 1913,
the *New York Times* carried a piece with the following headline:

BIG PORTSMOUTH FIRE LOSS
$1,000,000 Damage and Two Deaths – Suffragettes Suspected.

The article began by saying: 'The suffragette 'arson squad' is popularly
credited with the starting of the great fire in the dockyard here
Saturday night. It is recalled that when the headquarters of the militants were raided, papers were discovered disclosing a design to fire
the yard'.

The inquest into the deaths of Pensioner Chief Yeoman Pook and
Signalman Stewart opened on 31 December and it was immediately

obvious who was suspected of causing the death of the two sailors. Sir Thomas Bramsdon, the coroner, heard evidence that 60 men and 30 women worked in the sail loft, where the fire was thought to have started. He asked, 'What class of women are they?' On being reassured that many were the widows of servicemen and hearing a little about the working conditions at the dockyard, it seemed that some of the jurors still had their suspicions. One enquired of the foreman who was giving evidence, 'What means have you of checking the women coming in?'

There was some discussion about whether it would have been possible for any woman to slip in without being identified. Another juror then asked, 'If I was at the dockyard that night and wanted to set fire to it, could I have got into it?' He was assured that this would not have been possible. Later on, the idea that a woman could have entered the dockyard disguised as a naval officer was raised. The prevailing mood was that a woman had started the fire.

The whole of the inquest was concerned with the question of women being able to gain access to the dockyard and the impossibility of any outsider getting in to start a fire. Although no link was ever conclusively established, the general belief was that this had all the hallmarks of another arson attack by the WSPU. The verdict of the jury was that the two dead sailors had died from suffocation, which was indisputably true. They further said that there was no strong evidence to show how the fire had started. During the inquest, an Admiralty chemist had mentioned that a pile of hemp from ropes could catch fire spontaneously, under the right circumstances. He gave as an example, the heat of the sun being so great as to start a fire. This struck everybody as being singularly unlikely in the middle of December and the jury specifically declined to accept this theory.

The balance of possibilities suggests that the fire at Portsmouth was the work of suffragettes. It was, however, in nobody's interests for anyone to be pursued, let alone convicted, for the blaze. It would have put the government in the most terrible position if a woman was sentenced to death for an attack like this.

What was going on in the wider political scene at this time? The National Union of Women's Suffrage Societies had formed an alliance with the Labour Party and were lending it their support at by-elections. The NUWSS had the previous year established the Elections Fighting Fund Committee, whose aim was to raise money and offer support to Labour candidates during elections. Partly as a reward for this support, the Labour Party had agreed at their 1913 conference not to support any change in the franchise unless it included the vote for women. This neat politicking on the part of the NUWSS was in sharp contrast to the attitude of the WSPU, who refused to have any dealings with the Labour Party and virtually regarded them as enemies.

The Liberals were now in an unenviable position. They had, since the two general elections of 1910, relied upon Labour and the Irish Nationalists to give them a majority over the Conservatives in parliament. The Liberal government had already had to offer various concessions to the Irish Nationalists as the price for their continued support, now what if the Labour Party were to demand an extension of the franchise to working men and women as their price for backing the Liberals in parliament? Plainly, Millicent Fawcett and her NUWSS were playing a very shrewd game and a far more productive one politically than the stance which the WSPU had adopted.

The fiction is maintained, whenever suffragette violence is mentioned, that great care was taken by those initiating attacks to ensure that nobody was hurt in the process. Two bombings carried out in January, 1914, should alone be sufficient to give the lie to this assertion.

At 8.00 pm on Wednesday, 7 January 1914, in the city of Leeds, an explosion took place which was so loud that it was heard across the entire city. It had taken place at the Harewood Territorial Army Barracks in Woodhouse Lane, one of the main streets of the city. The barracks were being used as a temporary police base at the time of this incident. It was a miracle that nobody was seriously hurt by the dynamite bomb which was lobbed over the wall of the barracks, landing near the canteen. A caretaker was cut by flying glass when all the windows in the nearby buildings were blown in. A near casualty was Sergeant-Major Payne of the West Riding Ambulance Corps. He was sitting in his office and the blast knocked him off his chair.

The attack on the barracks was the second bomb to explode in Leeds in the space of 24 hours. The night before, an electricity generating station in the Crown Point district of the city was damaged by high explosives. Although no responsibility for these two attacks was claimed by the WSPU, it is hard to know who else could have been to blame. The suffragettes were the only terrorist group operating in Britain at that time.

In 1873, an enormous glasshouse was opened at the Glasgow Botanic Gardens. It was a fantastic structure, with a 150-foot-wide dome, made up of small panes of glass. This was called the Kibble

Palace, after the man responsible for its construction and soon became a landmark in the city. Both Benjamin Disraeli and William Gladstone were, at different times, installed as rectors of Glasgow University, both events taking place in the Kibble Palace.

In the early hours of 24 January 1914, the watchman employed to keep an eye on the Kibble Palace at night and protect it from thieves or vandals, was making his rounds of the building. He checked that nobody was in the Botanic Gardens after dark and that nothing was amiss. His work entailed nothing more arduous than chasing the occasional adventurous teenager out of the gardens. This night though, was due to be different. As he patrolled the outside of the glass palace, he spotted something very odd. It was a sputtering length of string. When he bent down to investigate, he found to his horror that this was a fuse, attached to a bomb. Instead of fleeing in panic, the man took out a penknife and calmly severed the fuse, thus rendering the bomb harmless.

As the night-watchman stood up, he must have been congratulating himself on a narrow escape. At that moment, a second bomb exploded nearby, with devastating force, shattering the sides and roof of the great glasshouse. It was the closest of shaves for the man, who fortunately had his back to the explosion, which showered him with fragments of broken glass. Investigation of the scene in daylight provided a chilling insight into the minds of those responsible for the attack on the Kibble Palace. A woman's veil was found, together with an empty champagne bottle and the remains of some cakes. Footprints indicated the presence of at least two women.

Whoever had planted the bombs had sat, eating and drinking, waiting for the best opportunity to strike. They must have seen the watchman on his rounds, knowing perfectly well that somebody was walking around the glasshouse. Setting off two explosions under such circumstances shows that those who lit the fuses did not care at all if this man was injured or even killed by their actions. Later that year, Marion Crawford, a prominent member of the WSPU, was sent to prison for two years for this attack, she was lucky not to have faced a charge of murder.

Less than a fortnight after the bomb attack in Glasgow, three country houses were attacked in Perthshire, two burned to the ground and the third severely damaged, but not wholly destroyed by the fires which were started. Once again, the suffragettes showed a complete disregard for the lives of others.

The owner of Aberuchill Castle was not in residence at the time, but a number of domestic staff was living on the premises, in quarters at the top of the house. By great good fortune, the alarm was raised and they were able to escape, but the scenario could have turned out very differently. In modern histories of the suffragettes, this kind of activity is almost invariably dismissed casually as an attack on an 'empty house'.

The terrorist attacks of the suffragettes were becoming more and more erratic and irrational. Why anybody would imagine for a moment that blowing up a greenhouse would lead to the extension of the franchise is something of a mystery. Even by the standards of the WSPU though, the next attacks in February 1914 were baffling.

In 1906, a Carnegie public lending library was opened in Northfield, a suburb of Birmingham. It was hugely popular with local people. At 2.00 am on 12 February 1914, the library was broken into and a fire started. Within a few hours, the building was gutted: the roof had fallen in and the library was a smoking ruin. When dawn came, a piece of paper was found attached to the railings at the back of the building. It proclaimed, 'Give Women the Vote'. Nearby was a parcel, which when opened proved to contain a copy of a book by Emmeline Pankhurst. Inscribed in this was the message: 'To start your new library'. Much anger was generated locally against the suffragettes by this singularly pointless act of vandalism.

On the same night that the library at Northfield was burned to the ground, a bomb was planted at the home of Arthur Chamberlain. Moor Green Hall was a mansion near Birmingham and somebody had broken in and left a bomb, which was supposed to be triggered by a burning candle. Fortunately, this primitive timing mechanism failed to set off the explosives.

The church of St Mary's in the tiny Scottish village of Whitekirk, is one of the most ancient in Scotland. Dating from the 1100s, it was in medieval times a site of pilgrimage. It seems inconceivable that anyone could wish to damage such a place, but a little over a week after the library at Northfield had been destroyed, a suffragette squad arrived at St Mary's Church in the middle of the night and burned it down. A photograph taken the day after the fire shows the church a smouldering wreck, with the roof having fallen in and all the windows blown out by the heat. We can only imagine what the residents of the village felt about the loss of their beautiful old church and the feelings aroused against those who had carried out such a vindictive act.

On the first day of spring, the terrorists turned their attention once more to London. In 1914, the rector of the Church of St John the Evangelist, Westminster was the Venerable Albert Wilberforce, Archdeacon of Westminster and Chaplain to the House of Commons. Perhaps it was his connection with parliament that led to his church being targeted by the suffragettes. If so, then the terrorists were making a grave mistake as the Venerable Wilberforce was an outspoken supporter of women's suffrage. Half an hour after the end of the evening service at St John's, on Sunday, 1 March, a bomb exploded in the gallery. Stained glass windows were blown out and a number of pews were destroyed. This was the first of a number of bombs aimed at churches in central London.

By the beginning of spring 1914, the WSPU had been reduced to the status of a very small militant group, rampaging around the United Kingdom and attacking increasingly peculiar targets, such as greenhouses, libraries and churches. The idea of 'social purity', which was becoming an obsession with both Emmeline and Christabel Pankhurst, could only have the effect of alienating still more potential supporters of the WSPU. The only thing that the group really had going for it was the input of wealthy donors who were paying the wages of the terrorists and so enabling them to continue their activities. The WSPU would struggle on for another six months, but it was really dead on its feet, disliked by many of the general public, viewed with detestation by the main political parties and regarded as a positive nuisance by the moderate suffragists who were making great strides by working patiently with sympathetic members of the Liberal and Labour parties.

The one thing that the WSPU did have though was money. The spectacular attacks, which attracted so much attention, also prompted various rich women to send more money to Mrs Pankhurst. Overall membership numbers might be dwindling, but those who remained in the organisation were still ready and willing to conduct further terrorist attacks. The fact that their activities were now acknowledged even by other suffragists as harming the cause, made not the slightest difference. The bombings and arson continued.

Chapter Nine

Dead End – Saved by the War

❝ ... through the action of a certain class, the suffrage question is as dead as Queen Anne. ❞

(Philip Snowden, Chancellor of the Exchequer, speaking after suffragettes attempted to bomb Westminster Abbey in June 1914)

The evening service at St Martin-in-the-Fields on Sunday, 5 April 1914, was unexceptional. It was later remembered that one of the worshippers had been a fashionably dressed young woman, but there was nothing unusual about her to excite suspicion. After the service, which ended at 9.10 pm, the church, in London's Trafalgar Square, was closed as usual. At precisely 10.30 pm, the windows on the south side of St Martin-in-the-Fields were blown out by an explosion, covering passers-by with broken glass. Smoke began billowing out of the shattered windows, showing that the explosion had started a fire.

When the fire brigade attended the scene and gained access to the church, they found that a considerable amount of damage had been caused to the interior of one of London's most famous churches. In addition to the broken windows, lights had been broken, woodwork set on fire and even the ceiling had been pockmarked and chipped when the bomb went off.

The attack on St Martin-in-the-Fields was the opening shot in the final stage of the suffragettes' terrorist campaign. Two days earlier, three small bombs had exploded at Belmont Church in Glasgow, but this had attracted little attention. An explosion in London was a far surer way of getting people to sit up and take notice.

On 17 April there were a number of serious fires, at least one of which was triggered by a bomb, a favourite tactic of the suffragettes. The Britannia Pier in Yarmouth, on the east coast of England, had an imposing pavilion and ballroom. This was 140 feet long, with a tower 80 feet high. It was a local landmark. At 4.00 am on 17 April, the two nightwatchmen on the pier heard a loud explosion, which they thought might be a warning maroon from a lighthouse or ship. However, within a few minutes the pavilion was ablaze.

Strong winds fanned the flames, which quickly reduced the ballroom to ashes. Iron girders twisted and buckled in the heat and by dawn, the pier had been destroyed. With daylight, the beach and gardens near the pier were found to be strewn with suffragette handbills and other literature. A postcard was also found, on which was written, 'Votes for Women. Mr McKenna has nearly killed Mrs Pankhurst. We can show no mercy until women are enfranchised.' The assumption was that a bomb had been planted in the concert hall and probably surrounded by cans of oil and other inflammable material.

The fire at Yarmouth was one of a number that took place that day. In Kingston Upon Thames, a music hall was so severely damaged that the roof caved in; a lino factory in Staines was destroyed; a skating rink and laundry in Penzance were burned down; and 15 horses were killed in a fire at a farm near Kelso. It is impossible to say which of these other fires were attributable to the suffragettes, but many newspapers reported them together with the bomb attack on Yarmouth pier as being all of a piece.

From time to time, the suffragettes attempted to cause floods by exploding bombs on canals or aqueducts. The explosion on the bank of the Stratford-on-Avon canal near Birmingham in 1913 could have been disastrous, but it was not the worst or potentially most damaging attack of that kind. That took place on the night of Saturday, 2 May 1914. The consequences had this particular bomb gone off, would have been almost unimaginable. The Upper Windleden Reservoir, near to the Yorkshire town of Penistone, contained almost 140 million gallons of water. Below it, was another, smaller reservoir, the Lower Windleden Reservoir. The flow of water from the larger reservoir was controlled by a valve house, through which the water ran along a conduit. A workman checking this conduit on Sunday, 3 May, found a large iron pipe filled with explosives, which had been laid near the foot of the valve tower. It would not have been easy to plant this device as it would have entailed wading through running water for a hundred yards or so.

The fuse for this bomb had been a wax taper, which had gone out before it reached the charge. What the result would have been if an explosion had actually taken place at that part of the reservoir, was succinctly summed up in the *Manchester Guardian*:

> *Had the bomb exploded and seriously damaged the valve tower, the rush of water would probably have displaced the surrounding masonry, and the whole 138 million gallons of water in the reservoir would have swept down the valley into the smaller Lower Windleden Reservoir. The banks at the lower end of this might then have given way under the pressure, and had this occurred the whole of the contents of the two reservoirs would have been released into the valley below.*

An engineer for the Dewsbury and Heckmondwike Water Board said that whoever planted the charge knew exactly where the greatest damage could be caused with the least force. This was not just a symbolic protest, but a deliberate attempt to flood an entire valley, with all the consequent damage and loss of life that this would result in.

Another London church was the target for the next bomb attack. The Metropolitan Tabernacle in London's Elephant and Castle is famous for its association with the preacher, Charles Spurgeon. On the afternoon of Sunday, 10 May a bomb exploded in the gallery of this church, causing some structural damage. A placard was found nearby, which proclaimed, 'Put your religion into practice and see that women obtain their freedom'. A suffragette called Annie Bell was later charged with this bombing.

The spate of bombings and arson had alarmed the authorities in some cities so much that they had instituted patrols to check for bombs on railway lines and other public places. Some people considered such precautions pointless, but they proved their worth in Glasgow on 22 May. Half of Glasgow's water supply was carried into the city from Loch Katrine via a huge aqueduct. One night one of these watchmen was walking along the pillars that supported the aqueduct, checking that all was well. He came across an area of freshly dug earth, which naturally aroused his suspicions. Further investigation showed that two bombs had been buried at the base of one of the columns supporting the aqueduct. The fuses had actually been lit, but thankfully had gone out. Nearby, was a woman's handbag, two trowels and the latest copy of *The Suffragette*. The possible consequences of half the water supply to the second largest city in Britain being cut off were truly horrifying. It seemed to those interested in such matters that although the WSPU was declining as a political force, they still had the ability to cause a great deal of harm unless they were stopped.

Throughout June 1914 the saga of the WSPU and their bombing campaign was moving inexorably towards a wholly unexpected resolution. It appears – from evidence in the newspapers, from the fact that membership figures were declining, and from the angry response from the general public when they tried to hold public meetings – that the suffragettes were deeply unpopular. However, they still attracted financial backers, had plenty of money, as well as access to explosives, and there were still eager volunteers ready to undertake arson attacks and plant bombs. Two examples in early June will give an idea of how the campaign was continuing.

Early on the morning of Friday, 5 June 1914, a policeman found a metal pipe full of gunpowder in the entrance of Dudhope Castle, a mansion not far from Dundee. A fuse was attached to one end and was wrapped round a candle. This had been lit, burning down part way, but it was then presumably blown out by the wind.

At about the same time that the bomb was planted at Dudhope Castle, an explosion was heard in the village of Breadsall in Derbyshire. Shortly afterwards, the very old Church of All Saints was seen to be on fire. The fire brigade was summoned from Derby and the villagers did what they could, but the church was entirely gutted by the fire and by morning, the church had burned to the ground. No suffragette leaflets were found after the attack, but a hairpin was discovered near a small window, where it was thought the church might have been broken into. As previously noted, the finding of hairpins in this way was often a hallmark of suffragette attacks. There was a curious sequel to the attack on the church in Breadsall. Two years later a former suffragette was convicted of plotting to murder Lloyd George and evidence was given that she had also boasted of destroying the church.

All Saints in Breadsall was the second church to be wholly destroyed by fire in the early hours of 1 June 1914. At 3.00 am a fire began which left only the walls standing of the parish church at Wargrave, near Reading in Berkshire. The roof caved in and the bells fell from the tower. No glass was left in any of the windows and all the interior fittings were reduced to ashes. Postcards bearing suffragette messages, such as, 'To the Government Hirelings and women torturers' were found in the churchyard.

Financially, the WSPU had never been in better shape that summer. The group's income in the year up to February 1914 was the highest it had ever been. The increasingly strange targets of the arsonists and bombers had done nothing to discourage the wealthy backers, who were prepared to donate thousands of pounds to the suffragette cause. Asquith and his Home Secretary, Reginald McKenna, were both well aware that the key to suppressing the WSPU and ending their terrorism lay in hitting at those who were encouraging the suffragettes by handing over large sums of money. A plan was accordingly formulated to take action against these shadowy individuals.

At 5.30 pm on 11 June, the Home Secretary rose in the House of Commons to outline the government's new strategy for dealing with the suffragette attacks. He began by explaining that although the number of incidents overall was declining, those that did take place were increasingly serious. Mckenna talked of the 'sinister figures with money bags' who selected dupes and paid them a pound or two a week to carry out attacks and go on hunger strikes. The authorities now had enough evidence to bring a test case of civil action for damage to property and also criminal prosecutions for inciting violence.

There now occurred one of those strange coincidences that would not be out of place in a play or film. The Home Secretary was speaking in calm, measured tones about the sensible policies of the Asquith administration and how these were sure to triumph in the long run. He explained that the government was taking, 'patient and determined action'. No sooner were the words out of his mouth than there came the sound of an explosion. Another bomb had gone off, this time near to the Houses of Parliament. A number of MPs jumped to their feet and hurried from the chamber to investigate.

In nearby Westminster Abbey, tourists were heading towards the exits, the abbey was due to close at 6.00 pm and it was now a quarter to. There had been what witnesses described as 'a terrific explosion' and then a column of smoke and dust rose from the chapel where the coronation chair was kept and slowly spread through the rest of the abbey. The chair, on which monarchs have sat during their coronations since 1300, was slightly damaged by the bomb, which was powerful enough to have chipped the stonework of the ceiling high overhead. The explosion was heard a long way down Victoria Street and even, as we have seen, in the Houses of Parliament.

The police sealed off Westminster Abbey after the bomb attack and arrested two women. They proved to be harmless Danish tourists and were soon released. Apart from some superficial marks on the walls and ceiling of the chapel in which the coronation chair was kept and a few bits of broken stone carving, there did not appear to be any serious consequences in the aftermath of the explosion. This was regarded as being extremely fortunate because the bomb had been packed with pieces of iron, obviously with the intention of causing as much damage as possible.

It was to be almost 40 years before the discovery was made that a another very ancient relic had been irreparably harmed by suffragettes. At Christmas, 1950, four Scots nationalists 'kidnapped' the Stone of Scone, which had been kept beneath the coronation chair for over 600 years and which had originally been brought to London after being captured from the Scots. The four students, who had hidden themselves in the abbey overnight, pulled the sandstone block from under the coronation chair where it rested. To their amazement, they found that it had been broken in half at some time in the past. It is likely that this was a result of the bomb which exploded nearby, almost 40 years earlier.

Apart from the obvious motive of wishing to prevent terrorist activity in the United Kingdom, the Prime Minister and Home Secretary had other good reasons for wishing to put an end to the arson and bombings being carried out by members of the WSPU. One fear was that if the terrorism continued, then members of the public would take matters into their own hands and undertake revenge attacks on the suffragettes. This was not a far-fetched idea and raised the spectre of lynch mobs on the streets of Britain. Events that took place in the days following the bombing of Westminster Abbey showed all too clearly that this was a genuine threat to public order.

On the same day that the bomb was planted in Westminster Abbey, there were two other suffragette attacks, both in Surrey. Reigate cricket pavilion was burned down and a determined attempt was made to set fire to an ancient church in the town of Chipstead. Three separate fires were started, by piling oil-soaked material against the wooden doors of the church. Fortunately, the rector, aided by local residents, managed to put out the fires before they caused much damage, but news of these other attacks did nothing to calm the hostility that many members of the public were now feeling towards the suffragettes. This hostility had nothing whatever to do with the principle of extending the franchise to women. It was simply anger at those responsible for conducting a campaign of random attacks which, if they continued, would inevitably end up in causing more pointless injury or death to innocent bystanders.

The government was right to fear public disorder if something was not done to put an end to the terrorist attacks. The mood of the country was running very strongly against the suffragettes and, by association, the very idea of women's suffrage was also becoming unpopular. The Sunday before the Westminster Abbey bomb, a number of public meetings were broken up by hostile crowds. At Hyde Park, the police had to rescue a speaker from the WSPU, when a very large and angry crowd assaulted her. At Hampstead, a mob seized two women and began dragging them towards a pond, with the intention of ducking them. Again, the police were forced to intervene. There was similar trouble at Clapham Common, when at a public, open air meeting one of the speakers made reference to bombs. She too, narrowly escaped violence. The situation became even more hazardous for the WSPU after the attack in the Abbey.

The day after the attacks in London and Surrey, some members of the WSPU tried to set up a stand at an agricultural show in Portsmouth. The reaction of those visiting the show was so violently antagonistic towards the sight of suffragette banners that a near-riot ensued, with the women being pelted with bottles and bricks. The police had to rescue the suffragettes and escort them to safety. A day later, there was a similar incident at nearby Southsea.

In London, suffragettes began distributing leaflets at a music hall in the East End and were roughly manhandled and ejected from the theatre. It was noticed that the women in the audience were displaying more dislike of the activists than the men. Two days later, suffragettes attempted to disrupt a service in Westminster Abbey, by standing up and shouting slogans. This was more than a little tactless considering that the Abbey was the very site of one of the latest outrages. The women were chased from the abbey and once again, the police were forced to protect them from the wrath of ordinary men and women who had had enough of terrorism.

On the evening of Saturday, 13 June, just two days after the explosion in Westminster Abbey, there was an attempt to hold a WSPU meeting on open ground at Palmers Green, a district of north London. One of those who helped to organise the meeting was Herbert Goulden, Emmeline Pankhurst's brother. A crowd gathered, not to hear the speeches of the suffragettes but rather to put an end to the event. Goulden was knocked to the ground and several women were assaulted. Eggs and flour were thrown at those taking part in the meeting. Even when, with the help of the police, Herbert Goulden was put onto a tram, the crowd followed and laid siege to his home. It was a riot in all but name. That same weekend, there were similar disturbances in Leicester and on Hampstead Heath, where a platform set up by members of the WSPU was broken up by the crowd and thrown in a pond.

These were by no means the only attacks on suffragette meetings during this period. In every case, the hostility of the crowds had been provoked by the planting of bombs and fire-raising. Shouts of, 'Incendiaries!' often greeted the WSPU activists when they tried to set up their stalls. The small matter of women's suffrage was forgotten in the outrage at the terrorism of the WSPU.

The aggressive behaviour of crowds towards WSPU speakers from April 1913 onwards has been twisted into another strand of the accepted legend of the suffragettes. Accounts of hostile mobs and photographs of angry men shouting at suffragettes from this time have been represented as evidence of the outrage and disapproval of men at the idea of women being given the vote. In other words, the impression is given that the faces in the photographs are contorted with fury at the thought of women being given the franchise. In fact, these are very often people who have been roused by the terrorism to which the country was being subjected. They would have been just as angry if those carrying out the violent attacks had been not middle-class women but anarchists or Irish bombers. The cause for which the bombing and arson was being carried out was irrelevant; people were infuriated to see churches and libraries wantonly destroyed and bombs being left in public places.

The anger being felt by ordinary people about terrorism is often misrepresented by modern writers on the subject. We are typically told that the suffragettes had to put up with ridicule and anger, the impression being given that these emotions had been aroused by the demands of female enfranchisement. More often than not, the anger directed against the suffragettes was a direct result of the terrorist attacks they were carrying out. It is seldom mentioned that those sent to prison were often women who had been convicted of bombing or arson.

Lloyd George summed up the case succinctly. As early as October 1913 he had told a deputation from the National Union of Women's Suffrage Societies that parliament's attitude to female enfranchisement reflected the mood of the country as a whole. Militancy, he said, had converted indifference to hostility. This was even more true in June 1914 than it had been in the previous autumn. Women's suffrage had become a disreputable cause for many, tarnished by the unending stream of terrorist attacks.

Fears of public disorder should the suffragettes continue to start fires and plant bombs were proving to be fully justified. Although preventing such outbreaks of violence would in itself be sufficient cause to crack down on the WSPU, Asquith had another, and at least to him, even more powerful motive for putting a stop to the militant actions of the suffragettes. His own position as Prime Minister and the chances of the Liberal Party forming the next government after the election, which was due the following year, were now endangered by the situation that had developed around female suffrage.

Despite his personal opposition to the introduction of parliamentary votes for women, Asquith knew that his own cabinet was evenly divided on the issue. In the Liberal Party as a whole, the question was far more clear-cut. The majority of Liberal MPs favoured the enfranchisement of women, as did the most of the rank and file members of the party. Even had he felt inclined to ride roughshod over the views of so many in his own party, there were good reasons not to do so. Like the Conservatives, the Liberals relied heavily upon the support of their female members. During elections, their help was invaluable. The Conservatives had the Primrose League and the Liberals had the Women's Liberal Federation. In recent years, the Women's Federation had declared in support of female enfranchisement and were refusing to work in support of any candidate at a by-election who would not pledge support for the parliamentary vote for women. Worse still, many women were defecting from the Liberals. Between 1912 and 1914, 68 branches of the Women's Liberal Federation folded up and 18,000 members resigned. Most had transferred their allegiance to the Labour Party.

At the last election, in December 1910, the result had been wafer thin, with the Liberals gaining 272 seats to the Conservative's 271. The loss of just a few seats at the next election could mean the difference between victory and defeat. As if this were not enough, Lloyd George had promised both Sylvia Pankhurst and the Labour MP George Lansbury that he would refuse to serve in a future Liberal administration that was not fully committed to extending the franchise to women. The idea of a Liberal government without the 'Welsh Wizard' was unthinkable.

Asquith knew in June 1914 that he had been outflanked on the question of women's suffrage. The Labour Party was officially committed to the introduction of universal adult suffrage, the Conservatives were sure to make some more limited offer of their own before the next election and the Liberal Party as a whole was entirely behind votes for women. It was time for a change of tack.

It is by no means unknown for politicians to change their views, even to execute a 180-degree turn on matters about which they have previously appeared to be most passionate. This is in the nature of politics and Asquith was probably quite ready to do an about-turn. There was only one obstacle now in the way of him changing his mind, becoming a convert to the principle of female emancipation, and announcing that the Liberals would go into the next election with a promise of granting the parliamentary vote to women. This barrier preventing the Prime Minister from announcing publicly that he had

had a change of heart and wished now to commit his party to extending the franchise to women, was of course none other than the Pankhursts and their suffragettes.

It is one thing for a politician to wriggle like an eel until he is facing the opposite direction. This is by no means an uncommon occurrence. It is another thing entirely for a Prime Minister to appear so weak and indecisive that a few arson attacks and terrorist bombings will be enough to force him to abandon a course of action or change radically the direction of the government which he leads. The consequences of this can be disastrous.

The bill granting Home Rule to Ireland was still moving forward, but in Ulster the Protestants were in open revolt. Two months before the Home Secretary announced his latest moves against the Women's Social and Political Union, enormous consignments of arms were landed in the north of Ireland at the ports of Larne and Bangor. These consisted of 24,000 rifles and 3 million rounds of ammunition. A provisional government had been formed in the province of Ulster and it was the intention to resist the imposition of Home Rule by armed force. There was considerable doubt that the army would be willing or able to prevent this and the government in Westminster was faced with the very real prospect of civil war breaking out in the United Kingdom.

If ever there was a time when a British Prime Minister needed to appear steadfast and resolute, thoroughly determined not to give in to the threat of violence, then the early summer of 1914 was that time. To give the impression of being intimidated by bombings or shooting would have been to send the worst possible message to the armed paramilitaries in Ulster; that here was a man who could be bullied and blustered into submission. For Asquith to appear in this character could have been enough to encourage the Ulster rebels into beginning an armed insurrection. A change of policy about women's suffrage was simply not possible if it should look for a moment as though it was the terrorist campaign that had persuaded Asquith to change his mind.

It was not only in Ireland that the Prime Minister's actions were being closely watched for any sign of weakness. The industrial unrest that had swept the country during the 'Great Unrest' of 1911 was still simmering away. A prime minister who was so scared of a few fires that he would surrender would have been something of a godsend to some of the more militant trade unionists.

On the international stage too, things were moving towards the greatest crisis of modern times, when the slightest sign of hesitation or lack of determination would be an open invitation for other countries to strike. When, in August, Germany invaded neutral Belgium, one of the calculations being made in Berlin was whether or not the British had the strength and determination to go to war for the sake of Belgium. In both Berlin and Belfast, Prime Minister Herbert Asquith was being closely watched for the least sign of weakness. For all these reasons, Asquith could not for a moment consider promising any sort of extension of the franchise to women until all militant actions had ceased for good. As soon as this had been achieved, then he could leave a decent interval, before explaining that he had been persuaded by those around him that it was time for a change.

Unfortunately, there seemed to be no sign at all that the militant suffragettes were planning to call a halt to their campaign. The Westminster Abbey bomb was detonated on the Thursday. The following Sunday saw the bombing of another church. Just after evensong, there was an explosion in St George's Church in Hanover Square. This place of worship in London's West End, was a popular location for society weddings. One man who had married there was former American president, Theodore Roosevelt. By coincidence, he was staying at the nearby home of an old friend, having arrived in London only the previous day. The explosion broke several stained glass windows, but did no other damage. The next day, a suffragette was caught with a bomb at the horse show taking place at Olympia.

It was not only the government that had tired of the suffragette militancy and realised correctly that it was preventing any progress on the gaining of women's suffrage. The Labour Party was officially committed to extending the franchise to women, but had no time at all for the WSPU and their increasingly mad and dangerous bids for publicity.

Speaking on the Saturday following the Westminster Abbey bomb, Philip Snowden, who would go on to become the first Labour Chancellor of the Exchequer, said uncompromisingly:

I do not believe that any cause can be promisingly advanced by immoral means. My record on the women's question is known to all of you. I totally disagree with the claim that militancy has advanced the cause. A year or so back there was the prospect of a measure passing the House of Commons, and I say now that, through the action of a certain class, the suffrage question is as dead as Queen Anne. There is not now a single member who has the heart to take up the question.

Snowden's own wife was a dedicated suffragist who also disapproved very strongly of the terrorist tactics the WSPU had adopted. Speaking herself a few months earlier, she had said that she would rather wait a hundred years for the vote, than see enfranchisement being achieved by methods which were themselves unjust, because they inflicted injury and suffering upon innocent people.

Asquith was caught in a position where making some sort of concession on suffrage would be very advantageous to him and his party at the next election and yet to make that concession would be political suicide while the terrorism continued. He and his Home Secretary redoubled their efforts to close down the WSPU and put a stop to the violence.

That the government was determined to prevent the suffragettes from being able to continue their violent campaign was clear from the actions taken by the police. On 23 May, Lincoln's Inn House, the WSPU headquarters in Kingsway, was raided again and Grace Roe, who was temporarily in charge, was arrested. A lot of papers were seized. The WSPU then moved to another office, in Tothill Street, near parliament itself. On 9 June, this too was raided by the police and more paperwork taken away. The next day, the suffragettes moved their headquarters again, this time to No. 2 Campden Hill Square in Kensington, the district where many of their wealthiest sponsors lived. They had no sooner settled in than the police arrived with another warrant and once again, papers were taken away. It was plain that there would be no let-up in the police attention.

In July, Sidney Drew, manager of the Victoria House Printing Company, was summonsed in connection with an edition of *The Suffragette* which he had printed. It was alleged that as a consequence of material published in the 2 January 1914 issue, he had been 'soliciting, inciting, and endeavouring to persuade divers women, members of the Women's Social and Political Union, and others to commit malicious damage to property'.

Drew was convicted of this offence at the Old Bailey in July and sent to prison for two months. It was very clear that the government was going to be pursuing anybody associated with or having any connection at all to the terrorists. At the same time, Asquith was putting out feelers with a view to striking some sort of deal with non-militant suffragists and signalling that he would be amenable to a change in the franchise in favour of women, if only the violence ended.

On 20 June, the Prime Minister agreed to meet a group of working-class women belonging to Sylvia Pankhurst's East London Federation. They explained to the Prime Minister that their views would only be respected if they had the vote. After listening carefully to what these women had to say, Asquith gave the clearest hint yet of the direction in which his mind was moving on this subject. According to Sylvia Pankhurst, he said, 'If the change has to come, we must face it boldly and make it thoroughgoing and democratic in its basis'. This indicates that the Prime Minister was probably thinking in terms of universal franchise. After all, working women like this would be sure to vote for either his party or Labour, with which he was allied.

Eight days after the meeting between the Prime Minister and representatives of the East London Federation, an event took place in Eastern Europe which was ultimately to bring the suffragette campaign to an abrupt end. Archduke Franz Ferdinand and his wife were shot dead in the Bosnian town of Sarajevo by a young Serbian terrorist, an action that eventually led to the First World War.

July saw almost the last of the attacks by the militants of the WSPU. A couple of these were exceedingly odd. On 8 July, for instance, came the attempted bombing of one of the most unlikely targets imaginable. Just before dawn, the nightwatchman at the cottage where Robert Burns was born, not far from the Scottish town of Ayr, heard a noise outside the cottage. He discovered two women placing bombs against the wall of the building. He managed to detain one, although her companion escaped. The bombs were very large, each containing over 8 lbs of blasting powder. Twenty-foot fuses were attached to the devices. It is fortunate for the watchman that he came out when he did, because such a quantity of explosives would have been enough to demolish the building and kill anybody within.

There were three further terrorist incidents on 12 July, one of which caused serious injury. A bomb exploded in a mailbag on a train travelling between Blackpool and Manchester. Since the suffragettes had been in the habit of sending letter bombs made from phosphorous through the post, it was assumed that they were responsible for the fire caused in the mail van. Six sacks of mail caught fire and this in turn set fire to the wooden carriage of the train in which they were travelling. A guard was severely burned while extinguishing the flames.

The same day that the train en route to Manchester was set alight by an explosion, a group of militants in Leicester were preparing to attack another part of the railway system. On the London and North Western line, between Leicester and Nuneaton, is the small station of Blaby. In 1914, it was an out-of-the-way spot, where nobody was likely to be around in the early hours of the morning. There were four members in the arson squad who carried cans of naphtha solution to the little station. They began a number of fires, with the result that all the buildings on the 'down' side of the tracks were destroyed, including the ticket office. At the scene, they left suffragette literature, so that nobody would be in any doubt about the motive for the attack.

It is fascinating to look at the subsequent stories of some of those eager young firebrands in later years. One of the women who burned down Blaby Station was Elizabeth Rowley Frisby, whose father was a prominent Leicester businessman. During the First World War, Elizabeth Frisby did a lot of work with the YMCA, for which she was awarded the MBE. After the war, she joined the Conservative Party and in 1927 was elected a member of the City Council. In the same year, she was also appointed a Justice of the Peace. In 1941, she became Lord Mayor of Leicester, the first woman to hold the post.

In March 1914, a bomb had exploded in the Church of St John the Evangelist in Smith Square, Westminster. Whether coincidentally or not, just round the corner from this church was the house of Home Secretary Reginald McKenna. After the bomb attack, worshippers at the church had been on the alert in case another attempt was made to damage their church. This vigilance paid off, because at the evening service on 12 July, a middle-aged woman was noticed to be behaving in a very strange and furtive manner. As she left at the end of the service, a regular worshipper called Alice Oakley noticed, to her alarm, a flame burning beneath the pew that the other woman had just vacated. She asked the woman if she had perhaps forgotten something. Not receiving a satisfactory reply, Miss Oakley then told Mrs Washbourne, the Deaconess and also the sacristan, Mr Walker.

While the alarm was spreading in this way, the woman who was the object of such suspicion had hurried out of the church and was heading across Smith Square. What nobody knew was that she had been tailed to the church by plainclothes detectives, because she was the chief suspect in another recent bombing of a church, that of the Metropolitan Tabernacle in south London. The detectives arrested her when they saw the uproar in the church she had just left.

In the church, the congregation was left to deal with the problem of a large bomb which had a burning candle sticking out of the top. It was carried out onto the steps, and buckets of water thrown over it until the candle was out and the gunpowder thoroughly saturated. As previously noted the rector of the church, Archdeacon Wilberforce, had for many years been an outspoken advocate of women's suffrage.

The woman arrested for planting the bomb at St John the Evangelist turned out to be Annie Bell, who was very well-known to the police. As well as being charged in connection with planting the bomb on 12 July, she was also charged with being responsible for the explosion at the Metropolitan Tabernacle. In court, the explosives expert from the Home Office gave evidence that the bomb at Smith Square had contained 5½ lbs of gunpowder, making it large enough to have caused a lot of damage and killed quite a few people had it gone off.

Many of the suffragette bombers were dangerous and determined. We have looked in some detail at the behaviour of both Emily Davison and Jennie Baines, both of whom were in some ways exceedingly odd and exhibited a desire to cause harm to other people. Annie Bell was of the same stamp, although her conduct was even more peculiar. Were it not for the fact that she thought she was fighting for a good cause, one might perhaps believe that she was a little unbalanced.

At a demonstration outside Holloway Prison on 22 April 1913, Annie Bell screamed out, to nobody in particular, 'If any man interferes with me, I have a revolver and will use it!' This was more than enough for the police, who quickly arrested and searched her. She had been telling the truth, for she did indeed have in her pocket a fully loaded revolver. She had also a firearms certificate which meant that the weapon was legally in her possession, but the police were still not happy about somebody carrying arms like that during a protest. They confiscated the gun.

At various times during 1913, Annie Bell was arrested and fined trifling sums for obstruction and similar offences. She always refused to pay these, preferring to go to prison. The police began to watch Bell and follow her round unobtrusively. They believed that she was an active terrorist and they were quite right.

So strange was Annie Bell's conduct in court, after she had been arrested for the bombing of the two churches, that observers began to doubt her mental state. At her first appearance in the magistrates court, she lay down and asked for a pillow. As she was leaving the court to be remanded, she said to the magistrate, 'Goodbye, you paid bully'. Her behaviour at the next stage, her committal to the Old Bailey, was even more odd. She sang the *Marsellaise*, shouted and constantly interrupted the proceedings.

An alarming fact soon emerged about Annie Bell; she had been released from prison on licence, after going on hunger strike. That somebody could walk free of prison just by refusing to eat for a few days and then carry out bombings in this way was disturbing. It also brought the law into disrepute, because it meant that whatever the crime, suffragettes were essentially exempt from serving their sentence. Little wonder that the prisons had begun force-feeding again.

Rosslyn Chapel, more properly known as the Collegiate Chapel of St Matthew, is perched upon a hill outside Edinburgh. Built in the fourteenth century, it has become famous in recent years for its supposed connections to Freemasonry, the Knight's Templar, Holy Grail and various other fringe interests. In 2003 it featured prominently in the conspiracy thriller, *The Da Vinci Code*. So much has been written about this small church and yet few people seem to be aware that it was the site of one of the last suffragette bombings. On Monday, 13 July, a canister full of gunpowder was placed on the ledge of one of the windows of the chapel and then set off by means of a long fuse. Only superficial damage was caused to some of the stonework.

The police efforts to suppress the WSPU were becoming increasingly successful as the month went on. The headquarters were raided again and Grace Roe, the General Secretary, was arrested for possession of explosives. The publisher of their newspaper, *The Suffragette*, had been sent to prison for two months for inciting violence. The suffragettes were almost finished as a force to be reckoned with.

The repercussions of the assassination of the Archduke in Sarajevo continued to reverberate across Europe throughout July 1914. On 23 July, the Austro-Hungarian government sent an ultimatum to Serbia, whom they blamed for Franz Ferdinand's death. When no satisfactory response was forthcoming, Austro-Hungary declared war on Serbia on 28 July. This led to Russia mobilising its army two days later.

The very last bomb attack carried out by the suffragettes was in Ulster. On the morning of Saturday, 1 August 1914, a bomb exploded outside Lisburn's Christ Church Cathedral. The blast left a crater four feet deep, blew out a 300-year-old stained glass window and shattered masonry. The next day, police raided the home of a well-known local suffragette and arrested four women found there. It was not only in England that there was deep hostility towards the suffragette bombers. A crowd gathered outside the house in which the women had been arrested and as they were led out they were pelted with stones and mud. The windows of the house were also broken.

When the women arrested for their involvement in the explosion at the cathedral were taken to court, they were granted bail. However, because local feeling was running so high over the damage to the cathedral, they were taken to the railway station and put on a train to Belfast. News had travelled before them and when the train carrying them stopped at Lambeg, a crowd of women gathered there to denounce the suffragettes for their sacrilegious action. An angry mob was waiting for the train's arrival at Belfast and the police had to protect the women from attack.

On the same day as the bomb attack on Christ Church Cathedral, Germany declared war on Russia and then, two days later, on France. The First World War had begun. In the course of their attack on France, the German army had violated Belgian territory. Britain was pledged to defend Belgium and duly declared war on Germany on 4 August. Emmeline Pankhurst was in France at the time with Christabel, having just been released again under the 'Cat and Mouse Act'. As soon as Britain declared war, Mrs Pankhurst ordered the WSPU to suspend all activity. She and her daughter returned to their own country and ten days later the Home Secretary announced an amnesty and the unconditional release of all suffragette prisoners. The struggle between the suffragettes and Asquith's government came to an end by mutual agreement, with neither side winning nor losing.

There is no telling how the situation would have developed had war not come in the summer of 1914. Both sides were intractable and appeared unwilling to give an inch. As it was, Emmeline Pankhurst quickly lost interest in the struggle for women's suffrage, throwing her energies into the fight against Germany. She showed no further enthusiasm for the subject of votes for women and it was left to the moderate suffragists to negotiate the deal which eventually led to the enfranchisement of at least some women.

The extent to which the Pankhursts changed their view about matters may be seen in a statement made by Emmeline, when giving evidence during a court case, which we shall examine in the next chapter. For over a decade David Lloyd George had been the arch enemy of the suffragettes. Speaking of this same man in 1917, Mrs Pankhurst said that: 'We declare that there is no life more valuable to the nation than that of Mr Lloyd George. We would endanger our own lives, rather than his should suffer'. How times had changed!

Chapter Ten

The Plot to Kill the Prime Minister

We will hang Lloyd George from a sour apple tree.

(Coded letter from Alice Wheeldon,
produced at her trial in 1917)

Many suffragettes reserved a special place of loathing in their hearts for David Lloyd George, Chancellor of the Exchequer and later Prime Minister. This was a little odd really, because he was a dedicated supporter of female suffrage. His real sin in the eyes of the suffragettes was his failure to endorse Emmeline Pankhurst's own, idiosyncratic vision of equal suffrage, meaning, during the years of suffragette militancy, a franchise largely restricted to the middle and upper classes.

Whatever the reason, he became the focus of a huge amount of venomous hatred from many members of the Women's Social and Political Union. Some of the actions directed against Lloyd George, we have already looked at – the bombing of his new house, the sending of explosives to him through the post and the attack by Emily Davison on an old man who had the misfortune merely to *look* too much like the Chancellor. For some former suffragettes, this detestation of Lloyd George lingered on, even after the Pankhursts had made their peace with him.

The Pankhursts might have become Lloyd George's friends and enthusiastically supported the fight against Germany, but there were some former suffragettes for whom this was a step too far. They did not subscribe to the bellicose patriotism of Emmeline and Christabel Pankhurst and still regarded Lloyd George as the devil incarnate. These were women who opposed the war on ideological grounds and hated Lloyd George all the more after 1914 for his role in organising the nation to support the military. While the Pankhursts and their supporters were handing out white feathers to men who were not in uniform, other former members of the WSPU were doing everything in their power to sabotage the war effort. One suffragette who felt this way was Alice Wheeldon, who lived in Derby.

We have already seen that some of the most dangerous suffragettes were willing and able to undertake actions which could result in loss of life: Emily Davison; Jennie Baines, who blew up the train near Manchester; Annie Bell, the woman who planted bombs in London churches. Alice Wheeldon was among this group.

Alice Wheeldon was 48 when the war began in 1914. She had been responsible for various arson attacks on behalf of the WSPU, including burning down the church at Breadsall on 5 June 1914. In 1916, she was running a second-hand clothes shop in Derby. She lived with two of her children, 25-year-old Hettie and 24-year-old William. Another daughter, Winnie, was married to a chemist called Alfred Mason and lived with him in Southampton. Alice Wheeldon's husband, William, was a commercial traveller and so infrequently at home.

At the end of 1916, the authorities had their eye on the Wheeldon household and suspected that they were the centre of an anti-war conspiracy. Specifically, it was thought that Alice Wheeldon and her children were sheltering deserters and conscientious objectors in their home. In 1916, the government brought in the Military Service Act, which meant that all able-bodied men aged between 18 and 41 would be required to join the army. Some men refused to do so on the grounds that military service went against their conscience and many of these men served in ambulance brigades, while others ended up in prison. When there was no more room for them in the prisons, the Home Office set up camps where they were held.

There is not the least doubt and nor did Alice Wheeldon subsequently deny it, that deserters from the army stayed at the Wheeldons' house. They were part of a network of people who tried to help such men leave the country. Her own son William was due to be called up and Mrs Wheeldon was desperately anxious to see him travel abroad and so avoid ending up in the trenches of the Western Front.

A section of MI5 heard about the activities of the women in Derby and despatched an undercover agent, Alex Gordon, to pose as a conscientious objector on the run from the police. Formerly a radical journalist, he was now being paid to work as an informer or possibly agent provocateur. His immediate superior was Herbert Booth. On 27 December 1916, Gordon, who went under a variety of aliases, arrived at Alice Wheeldon's house and asked to be sheltered as a conscientious objector. Mrs Wheeldon arranged for him to stay at another woman's house and then, a few days later, Gordon returned to Alice Wheeldon, accompanied by a man whom he introduced as 'Comrade Bert'. This was the MI5 agent Herbert Booth.

It is now that things become complicated and two very different versions of the events of the next month emerge at the subsequent trial at the Old Bailey. There was no dispute that Alice Wheeldon spoke in very disparaging terms about Lloyd George, who had by that time become Prime Minister. Indeed, she spoke so unflatteringly of him that at her trial, the prosecuting counsel claimed that she used 'language which would be disgusting and obscene in the mouth of the lowest class of criminal'. In reality this amounted to no more than describing Lloyd George as a 'bugger'. She also used the word 'bloody' fairly freely, which was unusual for a woman at that time.

While snooping around her home, Alex Gordon found that Alice Wheeldon communicated with others who shared her views of Lloyd George by means of a code. To decipher letters written in this code, it was necessary to know a key sentence, which was, 'We will hang Lloyd George from a sour apple tree'. Shortly after meeting Alex Gordon, Alice Wheeldon contacted her daughter Winnie in Southampton and asked for her to obtain some poison from her husband, who was lecturing in chemistry at that time. On 4 January 1917, Alfred Mason, Winnie's husband, sent four glass phials to Derby, two of which contained strychnine and two curare. At the end of that month, Alice Wheeldon, her daughters Hettie and Winnie and Alfred Mason were all arrested and charged with conspiring to murder the Prime Minister.

The trial of the Wheeldons and Alfred Mason opened at the Old Bailey on 6 March 1917. The case for the Crown, outlined by the Attorney General, Frederick Smith, was that a plan had been hatched to fire a dart tipped with the South American poison curare at Lloyd George as he played golf near his home at Walton Heath. It was, he alleged, also the intention of the conspirators to kill at the same time Arthur Henderson, a Labour member of the cabinet. It was for this reason that the poison had been obtained. According to statements from Alex Gordon and Herbert Booth, or Comrade Bert as the Wheeldons knew him, Alice Wheeldon had said that Lloyd George was 'the cause of millions of innocent lives being sacrificed. The bugger shall be killed to stop it'.

Herbert Booth also said that the Wheeldons had revealed a previous plot to assassinate Lloyd George – when the suffragettes were active before the start of the war – by smearing poison on a nail and then arranging for it to penetrate his boot. It was alleged that she had told Booth and Gordon that a member of the WSPU had taken a job at a hotel in order to put this plan into execution, but when Lloyd George had left suddenly it had come to nothing.

Herbert Booth made a convincing witness, as did the head of his department, Major William Lauriston Melville Lee. Notable by his absence though, was the man who had apparently uncovered this plot. Alex Gordon was not called to give evidence and this omission on the part of the crown was never properly explained. Emmeline Pankhurst was called to give evidence during the trial, in order to show that the suffragettes now regarded Lloyd George as a precious national asset, rather than a bogey man.

The defence alleged that Alex Gordon had set up the whole scenario. Rather than acting as an informant, he was the one who had instigated the obtaining of the poison. This had not been done, according to Alice Wheeldon and her daughters, to kill Lloyd George. It was part of a deal that she had struck with Alex Gordon, whereby she would help him in exchange for a favour which he had promised to do for her. In this version of events, Alex Gordon had told the Wheeldon's that a camp where conscientious objectors were being held was guarded by fierce dogs. He wished to free some prisoners from the camp and would need first to kill the guard dogs. If Alice Wheeldon could get hold of some poison from her son-in-law for this purpose, then he would help arrange for her son William to evade military service by travelling to America.

There was little to choose between the two stories on offer to the jury. On the one hand, it was perfectly plausible that a former suffragette arsonist had concocted a bizarre plan to dispose of the man whom many members of the WSPU had been indoctrinated to see as their main enemy in the fight for women's suffrage. On the other, it was equally possible that a shadowy secret agent had dreamed up an elaborate fantasy in order to increase his own importance.

The jury had no such doubts and took less than half an hour to bring in verdicts of guilty against Alice Wheeldon, her daughter Winnie and son-in-law Alfred Mason. Hettie Wheeldon was acquitted. Alice Wheeldon was sent to prison for ten years, Alfred Mason for seven and his wife Winnie for five. None served anything like their full sentences.

Predictably enough, Alice Wheeldon went on hunger strike almost immediately. She was forcibly fed for a time, but her health declined rapidly. On 27 December 1917, the deputy Medical Officer at Holloway Prison reported that her condition was worsening. Her pulse was weak and her heart unsteady. It was in nobody's interests for a former suffragette to starve to death in prison and on 29 December, Lloyd George interceded. He wrote to Home Secretary Herbert Samuel, urging that Mrs Wheeldon be freed. On 31 December, she was released from prison, only to die a little over a year later in the great influenza epidemic of 1919.

After the war had ended in November 1918, Prime Minister Lloyd George made it plain that he wanted the other two 'conspirators' to be freed and on 26 January 1919, Alfred Mason and his wife left prison. They had spent less than two years behind bars.

So what was the truth about the plot to kill the Prime Minister? In recent years, a campaign has been launched to have the case reviewed, with the intention of securing a posthumous pardon for the Wheeldons and Alfred Mason. Derby City Council have placed a blue plaque on the house where Alice Wheeldon and her family once lived to commemorate an, 'anti-war activist, socialist and suffragist' (see Plate 2). No mention is made of her being a would-be assassin of the prime minister! Perhaps the safest verdict to bring in, based upon the evidence as we have it, would be the Scottish verdict of 'not proven'.

The greatest irony of all is that at the very time when Alice Wheeldon might have been conspiring to murder him, Lloyd George was actually in the process of arranging the legislation which would grant women the parliamentary vote. It would be interesting to know the effect that his assassination might have had upon those plans.

Chapter Eleven

How the Vote was Won

❝ ... the heroic patriotism of the women workers during the war had now made their claim irresistible. ❞

(Lloyd George, writing after the granting of the vote to women in 1918)

At the outbreak of war in 1914 there seemed to be little prospect of women in the United Kingdom being given the parliamentary vote in the near future, and yet by 1916, there was cross-party agreement on the subject and even the Conservative-dominated Lords submitted tamely to passing a bill which gave over eight million women the vote.

When the war began in the summer of 1914, an election was due by the end of 1915. By 1915, however, the country was being governed by a wartime coalition and it would hardly have been possible to hold a general election with so many men fighting abroad. It was this that led to the need for an urgent reform of the franchise. As we have seen, for men the parliamentary vote was dependent on residence and property qualifications. Men had to have lived in the same place for a length of time before being able to register to vote. Since it was intended to hold an election as soon as the war ended, this would have meant, under the law as it stood, that all the soldiers and sailors returning home from active service overseas would effectively have been disenfranchised by virtue of their military service. Moreover, many of the young soldiers fighting in the trenches would not in any case have been entitled to vote, because they had been living with their parents and were not themselves householders.

Obviously, this was all absurd. Then again, what of those men who had been directed to carry out war work in another part of the country, rather than serving at the front? It would be unfair if they too were to be disenfranchised, just because they had served in factories and mines, rather than on the Western Front. This consideration of the men doing war work at home led some MPs to raise the question of the women who were doing exactly the same sort of work. Surely, it was only fair if they too should be given the vote? After all, they were doing the same work as men on behalf of their country.

We have examined a number of myths and misrepresentations about the struggle for female suffrage before the First World War. We come now to another of the dubious assertions that are often made – one presented in many books as an established fact – that women finally gained the vote because of the way the majority of them behaved during the war. It is sometimes claimed today, and it was certainly asserted during the First World War when the decision was being made, that women were eventually granted the parliamentary vote in this country because of the war work so many of them undertook. From this perspective, the franchise was awarded like a medal for all the labouring in munitions factories, nursing and working as bus conductors that women did, among many other things. This is almost certainly untrue.

Lloyd George wrote after the war that 'the heroic patriotism of the women workers during the war had now made their claim irresistible'. Asquith said at the time that it was the efforts made by women in support of the war that had changed his mind about female suffrage. Yet the majority of the war work was undertaken by women under the age of 30. For instance, there were almost a million workers in the munitions factories, all, at least officially, aged between 18 and 30; although in fact at some factories over 60 per cent of women were under 18. So, if it was really the case that the efforts of those young women in their twenties, who had been taking over the men's jobs while they were away on active service, changed Asquith's mind, then one would have thought that they would have been given the vote in 1918. They were not. They were, in fact, specifically excluded from the franchise, as it was only for women over the age of 30. This was in contrast to the voting age for men, which was 21 at that time.

The idea that women were granted the vote as a reward for their war work provided a convenient excuse for politicians who had opposed female suffrage. The main sticking point, the desire not to appear to be giving in to the threat of violence, had gone. The Lords had been tamed and with the passing of the Parliament Act could no longer block the legislative programme of the Commons. The mood in the Commons had long been in favour of female franchise and so, with the terrorism ended, the way was now clear.

Of course, there were some politicians, men like Asquith, who had fought for years against the principle of women being allowed to vote in parliamentary elections and for them, the excuse of war work was very handy. Such men might otherwise have felt a little foolish if, after having strongly opposed votes for women for a decade or so, they suddenly announced that they had been wrong about this all along! By citing the contribution of women to the war, they were enabled to make a *volte face*, claiming that circumstances had changed so dramatically that they had been forced to change their views.

Having capitulated to the demand for the female franchise, it was necessary only to work out the fine details. Nobody in parliament was keen to see every woman suddenly given the vote, if that were to happen, then women would at once become a majority of the electorate. Instead, the same process by which men had gradually been enfranchised over the last 80 years or so would be followed, so it would be done in stages.

In 1916, Asquith set up a Speaker's Conference on Electoral Reform. This consisted of backbench MPs from all the political parties. This committee hammered out a new framework for the franchise. Chaired by the Speaker of the House of Commons, the conference had 13 Conservative members, the same number of Liberals, 4 from the Labour Party and 4 Irish Nationalists. After meeting 26 times, they reported back to the Prime Minister in January, 1917. By that time, Asquith had resigned and been replaced by Lloyd George.

The National Union of Women's Suffrage Societies arranged for a delegation of women to put the case to the conference for female suffrage. Emmeline Pankhurst, whose ability to fall out with everybody with whom she came into contact was legendary, refused to attend on the grounds that women's suffrage was no longer an important issue, compared, that is, to winning the war. From 1914 onwards, Mrs Pankhurst seemed to lose all interest in women's suffrage. When a group of representatives from all the main suffrage societies went to Downing Street to make some final remarks on the proposed legislation, they in turn refused to have Emmeline Pankhurst as a member of their deputation.

Lloyd George accepted in full the recommendations of the Speaker's Conference, which were that practically all men over the age of 21 should have the vote, regardless of property qualifications. Some women, property owners, the wives of property owners and university graduates over the age of 30 should also be given the vote. By the end of the year, the Representation of the People Act had been passed by the Commons by 364 votes in favour to 23 against. The House of Lords, not wishing for another confrontation with the Commons, also passed the bill. It became law in February 1918.

When women were finally given the parliamentary vote, it was on the terms of neither universal nor equal suffrage. Nevertheless, it was a start and ten years later, the law was changed so that both men and women had the vote on equal terms.

If women were not really granted the vote as a reward for their war service, and the fact that younger women and many working-class women were not enfranchised makes it very likely that they were not, what was the real reason for the change of heart, even in men like Asquith? It is instructive to look at what was happening in other countries in the years prior to and immediately following the end of the First World War.

Before the start of the First World War, New Zealand, Australia, Finland, Norway and some states of the USA had already given the vote to women. During and after the war, many more countries were to do so: Denmark in 1915; Canada, Estonia, Latvia, Poland and Russia in 1917; Germany, Hungary and Lithuania in 1918; Austria, the Netherlands and South Rhodesia in 1919; Czechoslovakia, Albania and the USA in 1920; and Burma and Ireland in 1922. Looked at from this perspective, Britain's granting of the vote to some women in 1918 was simply a reflection of the trend that was sweeping the world. There had not been agitation for female suffrage in all the countries listed above, but this had not prevented the changes in the franchise being made.

At the outbreak of war in 1914, the question of women's suffrage was off the political menu, at least until the violence ended. Since the only people undertaking violent actions in connection with the franchise for women were the members of the WSPU and as they had called an immediate halt to their activities when the war began, there was no longer any obstacle to considering the extension of the franchise. Other countries had already taken this step and more were moving in that direction and it would be absurd for the United Kingdom to be left behind.

With not just major nations like the United States giving the vote to women, but even small countries like Burma and Albania, to say nothing of neighbouring Ireland, Britain would have looked pretty foolish and out of step with worldwide political trends, had she not made at least some gesture towards the enfranchisement of women after the end of the war. This was particularly so when we bear in mind that colonial countries such as Canada, New Zealand, Rhodesia, Burma and Australia were also part of this movement towards greater democracy. It would have looked decidedly odd, with the rest of the empire moving in this direction, if the Mother Country alone had held out against women's suffrage. By 1914, it was plain to most progressive and forward looking thinkers that women's suffrage was coming to the countries of Western Europe and North America sooner, rather than later. All that Britain did was to follow a trend.

In the next chapter, we will examine what effect, if any, the activities of the WSPU had upon the granting of the vote to women. For many years, it was taken as being almost axiomatic that votes for women were achieved as a result of relentless campaigning by various suffrage groups, most notably the suffragettes of the WSPU. It is curious though to note that women in other countries gained the vote at about the same time without extensive lobbying, let alone conducting campaigns of bombing and fire-raising.

The popular feeling today is strongly in favour of the Pankhursts and their suffragettes having played a crucial role in gaining the parliamentary vote for women. It is no exaggeration to say that for most people, it is probably indisputable that the suffragettes forced the government to grant votes for women. It is time to look at the systematic distortion of history which has taken place over the last century and to see how the suffragettes were transformed from a gang of dangerous terrorists into a radical, mass movement struggling peacefully for civil rights.

Chapter Twelve

Birth of a Myth

*❝ Mrs Emmeline Pankhurst inspired and led the
Militant Suffrage Campaign. ❞*

(Inscription on the statue of Emeline Pankhurst near the
Houses of Parliament)

We have seen how the Women's Social and Political Union waged a relentless campaign of bombing and arson in the years leading up to the First World War and that these actions were not carried out by a handful of mavericks, but rather consisted of a systematic offensive conducted under the direction and control of the organisation's leaders.

The majority of those planting bombs and starting fires were paid employees of the WSPU. It has also been established that the suffragette contribution to the struggle for female suffrage was at best irrelevant and most probably counterproductive, as it delayed rather than hastened the granting of the franchise to women. Despite this, the myth that the Pankhursts and their suffragettes were crucial to the gaining of votes for women is a powerful one, permeating our modern culture.

The mistaken notion that the suffragettes played an important role in the enfranchisement of women in this country goes hand in hand with another popular misconception – that the actions of Mrs Pankhurst and her suffragettes were largely non-violent, being limited to heckling, smashing windows and damaging letters. This particular aspect of the mythology surrounding the suffragettes was established very soon after the death of Emmeline Pankhurst in 1928.

The rehabilitation of Emmeline Pankhurst and her transformation from fanatical and irrational extremist to national treasure was extraordinarily swift. In May 1914, she was involved in a riot outside Buckingham Palace, in the course of which she was arrested. Just 16 years later, on 6 March 1930, a Conservative Prime Minister was making adulatory speeches at the unveiling of a statue of her in Victoria Tower Gardens, next to the Houses of Parliament. This put the official seal of approval on Mrs Pankhurst and her suffragettes and from that time onwards, up to the present day, questioning her legacy or saying anything uncomplimentary about either her or the women who followed her has been considered to be in rather poor taste.

Visiting that statue of Emmeline Pankhurst today is, incidentally, a rather disconcerting experience. 'Glorifying terrorism' is actually a specific criminal offence under the 2006 Terrorism Act, and yet an inscription on one of the low walls surrounding the statue's plinth says, 'These Walls and Piers have been erected in memory of Dame Christabel Pankhurst who jointly with her Mother Mrs Emmeline Pankhurst inspired and led the Militant Suffrage Campaign'. In other words, the aim of this structure, which stands in the shadow of the

Houses of Parliament, is to commemorate and celebrate Britain's first terrorist bombing campaign of the twentieth century.

The real puzzle is why, a century later, we are still happy to accept that the suffragettes were responsible for gaining the vote for British women and why their terrorist activities have been comprehensively brushed under the carpet. There are probably three main reasons for the enduring popularity of the suffragette mythos. The first of these is that even today, we still take the WSPU largely at its own estimation, viewing the propaganda generated by the group uncritically and regarding it, in many cases, as being historical fact.

Take, for example, that memorable slogan of 'Votes for Women'. As we now know, the aim of the WSPU was not 'Votes for Women' at all, but rather, 'Votes for university educated or property owning, female members of a certain social class', which does not sound nearly so catchy! There can be few people in this country unable immediately to identify the slogan, 'Votes for Women' and associate it with the suffragette movement. It is no small feat to coin a phrase of this sort which is still instantly recognisable a century later. The very words of this political catchphrase hint misleadingly that the franchise was being sought for 'women' as a group, and that the aim of the WSPU was the universal enfranchisement of women. As we have seen, this was not at all the case.

Then too, there are the visual images by which we know the suffragettes – the limp young woman in the jaws of a giant cat; the force-fed hunger striker; Emily Davison lying mortally wounded on the racetrack at Epsom – to give a few of the most powerful. These were all deliberately produced as propaganda and yet we take them today as summing up the movement for female enfranchisement in the early twentieth century. A photograph of a member of the National Union of Women's Suffrage Societies preparing a petition would not be nearly so striking, nor evoke the same emotions in us, even though her actions were ultimately to prove infinitely more effective.

Touching now upon the strange way that the memory of the suffragettes' terrorist attacks has faded from history, this seems to be in part an established trend with political violence that takes place very close to a major war. Two years after the end of the First World War, there was an IRA fire-raising campaign in England, which has been forgotten as completely as that of the suffragettes. In the summer of 1939, a matter of weeks before the outbreak of the Second World War, there was a series of bombing attacks in England, which ended with the death of five people in an explosion in the Midlands town of Coventry. This too is all but unknown today.

It seems that the wholesale slaughter of a world war tends to erase from the collective memory many dramatic incidents that took place in close proximity to the conflict. This is quite understandable. The small explosions caused by the suffragettes in 1913 and 1914 pale into insignificance when compared with the carnage on the Western Front or with the bombs dropped on London by Zeppelins in 1915.

The main reason though, that we are happy to accept the suffragette legend at face value, is probably that their story has those heroic and mythical qualities which so many of us find inspiring. It is history at its least complicated and most easily digestible. There are heroines, villains and suffering martyrs; it is based upon a simple narrative which ends, after a tremendous struggle, in the triumph of virtue. It has all the ingredients of a morality play. This is how we like our history to be: simple and straightforward.

There is something immensely attractive about these fables; they are a common feature in the popularly accepted history of Britain. Whether it is Emmeline Pankhurst fighting the hidebound and complacent political establishment, Florence Nightingale battling against the stupidity and sloth of the British army or Scott of the Antarctic engaged in a life or death struggle with nature, the idea of the lone, brave and good individual facing overwhelming odds and yet not being disheartened is one of our favourite images.

Of course, for myths of this sort to maintain their appeal, the heroes and heroines need to be demonstrably without fault and, like Caesar's wife, above suspicion. It is this that goes a long way towards explaining why the suffragette terrorism has been allowed to fade from view. We do not want those who appear to be on the side of the angels to be countenancing terrorist bombings against civilians. Unpalatable details are thus gradually stripped from the picture, leaving iconic figures whom we may unreservedly admire.

Once the public has been persuaded to take somebody to their hearts, such minor matters as whether they actually did anybody any good soon become trivial and hardly worth examining. Just as Florence Nightingale is the patron saint of nursing, so too is Emmeline Pankhurst universally revered as the person who gained the vote for women in this country. The facts of the case become less and less important as the years pass and we are left with men and women who appear to have no discernible faults at all.

This book has been an attempt to redress the balance a little and show another side to the Pankhursts and their suffragettes. That Emmeline and Christabel Pankhurst were both dedicated to their cause is not in doubt. The problem is that many people today do not apparently know just what this cause was and the extraordinary lengths to which the two women were prepared to go in order to achieve their end. If the Pankhursts deserve a place in the history of Britain, it is probably not for delivering the vote to women that they should be remembered, but rather for being the joint architects of the first terrorist campaign of the twentieth century to be waged in the United Kingdom.

Bibliography

Abrams, Fran, *Freedom's Cause, Lives of the Suffragettes* (London: Profile Books, 2003).

Adams, Jad, *Pankhurst* (London: Haus Publishing, 2003).

Atkinson, Diane, *Votes for Women* (Cambridge: Cambridge University Press, 1988).

Atkinson, Diane, *Purple, White and Green, Suffragettes in London, 1906–1914* (London: Museum of London, 1992).

Aylett, John, *The Suffragettes and After (Past in Questions)* (London: Hodder Education, 1988).

Boyd, Nina, *From Suffragette to Fascist, the Many Lives of Mary Sophia Allen* (Stroud: The History Press, 2013).

Bunyan, Tony, *The Political Police in Britain* (London: Julian Friedmann Publishers, 1976).

Burley, Michael, *Blood and Rage, a Cultural History of Terrorism* (London: Harper Press, 2008).

Cannon, John (Ed.), *The Oxford Companion to British History* (Oxford: Oxford University Press, 1997).

Colmore, G., *The Life of Emily Davison* (London: The Women's Press, 1913).

Cook, Chris; Stevenson, John, *Modern British History, 1714–2001* (Harlow: Pearson Education, 1983).

Fitzherbert, Claudia, *Emily Davison: The Girl Who gave her Life for her Cause* (London: Short Books, 2004).

Gilbert, Martin, *A History of the Twentieth Century* (London: Harper Collins, 2007).

Hattersley, Roy, *The Edwardians* (London: Little, Brown, 2004).

Hawksley, Lucinda, *March, Women, March* (London: Andre Deutsch, 2013).

Herbert, Michael, *'Up Then Brave Women': Manchester's Radical Women, 1819–1918* (Manchester: North West Labour History Society, 2012).

Kee, Robert, *Ireland* (London: Weidenfeld & Nicolson, 1980).

Liddington, Jill, *Rebel Girls: How Votes for Women Changed Edwardian Lives* (London: Virago, 2006).

Macdonald, Fiona, *Great Britons* (Great Bardfield: Miles Kelly Publishing, 2004).

Marlow, Joyce (Ed.), *Votes for Women* (London: Virago, 2001).

Marr, Andrew, *The Making of Modern Britain* (London: Macmillan, 2009).

Marriot, Emma, *Bad History* (London: Michael O'Mara Books, 2011).

Mayer, Annette, *The Growth of Democracy in Britain* (London: Hodder & Stoughton, 1999).

Meeres, Frank, *Suffragettes: How Britain's Women Fought and Died for the Right to Vote* (Stroud: Amberley Publishing, 2013).

Mitchell, Hannah, *The Hard Way Up* (London: Faber and Faber, 1968).

Morgan, Kenneth (Ed.), *The Young Oxford History of Britain & Ireland* (Oxford: Oxford University Press, 1996).

Palmer, Alan, *The Penguin Dictionary of Twentieth Century History* (Harmondsworth: Penguin Books, 1979).

Pankhurst, Sylvia, *The Suffragette Movement, an Intimate Account of Persons and Ideals* (London: Longman, 1931).

Perkin, Joan, *Victorian Women* (London: John Murray, 1993).

Pettiford, Lloyd; Harding, David, *Terrorism, the Undeclared War* (London: Arcturus Publishing, 2004).

Philips, Melanie, *The Ascent of Women, A History of the Suffragette Movement* (London: Abacus, 2004).

Pollard, Justin, *Secret Britain* (London: John Murray, 2010).

Powell, David, *The Edwardian Crisis, Britain, 1901–1914* (London: Macmillan, 1996).

Priestley, J.B., *The Edwardians* (London: William Heinemann, 1970).

Pugh, Martin, *The Pankhursts: The History of One Radical Family* (London: Vintage, 2008).

Pugh, Martin, *The March of the Women* (Oxford: Oxford University Press, 2000).

Purvis, June, *Emmeline Pankhurst: a Biography* (London: Routledge, 2002).

Purvis, June; Holton, Sandra, *Votes for Women* (London: Routledge, 2000).

Rayner, Ed; Stapley, Ron, *Debunking History* (Stroud: Sutton Publishing, 2002).

Robertson, Patrick, *The Shell Book of Firsts* (London: Ebury Press, 1974).

Robinson, Jane, *Bluestockings: The remarkable Story of the First Women to Fight for an Education* (London: Penguin, 2010).

Rubinstein, David, *Before the Suffragettes: Women's Emancipation in the 1890s* (London: Palgrave Macmillan, 1986).

Slee, Christopher, *The Guinness Book of Lasts* (London: Guinness Publishing, 1994).

Stanley, Liz; Morley, Anne, *The Life and Death of Emily Wilding Davison* (London: The Women's Press, 1988).

Steele, Philip, *Men, Women and Children in the First World War* (London: Wayland, 2010).

Tanner, Michael, *The Suffragette Derby* (London: Robson Press, 2013).

Taylor, A.J.P., *The First World War: An Illustrated History* (London: Hamish Hamilton, 1963).

Vallance, Edward, *A Radical History of Britain* (London: Little Brown, 2009).

Webb, Simon, *Dynamite, Treason and Plot, Terrorism in Victorian and Edwardian London* (Stroud: The History Press, 2012).

Williams, Anne; Head, Vivian, *Freedom Fighters* (London: Futura, 2007).

Williams, Brian, *Women Win the Vote, 6 February 1918* (London: Evans Brothers, 2005).

Index